DEFENSE OF ART

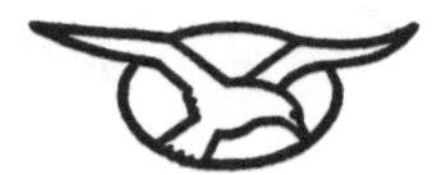

DEFENSE OF ART

CHRISTINE HERTER

W · W · NORTON & COMPANY

New York · London

Library of Congress Cataloging in Publication Data
Herter, Christine
Defense of Art by Christine Herter. New York.
W. W. Norton & Company, Inc., 1938.
Bibliography: p. 183-185.
1. Art.   2. Art Criticism.   3. Painting.   I. Title.

ISBN: 978-0-393-30036-9

W. W. Norton & Company, Inc., 500 Fifth Avenue,
New York, N.Y. 10110
W. W. Norton & Company Ltd. 37 Great Russell Street,
London WC1B 3NU

1 2 3 4 5 6 7 8 9 0

TO

PETERKIN AND SHAUGHRAUN

this book is dedicated
because
without their determined and joyous interruptions
it could never have reached completion

CONTENTS

PROLOGUE

"THIS Quarrel first began (as I have heard it affirmed by an old Dweller in the Neighborhood) about a small Spot of Ground, *lying* and *being* upon one of the two Tops of the Hill *Parnassus*; the highest and largest of which, had it seems, been time out of Mind, in quiet possession of certain Tenants, called the *Antients*; And the other was held by the *Moderns*. But, these disliking their present Station sent certain Ambassadors to the *Antients* complaining of a great Nuissance, how the Height of that part of *Parnassus*, quite spoiled the Prospect of theirs, especially toward the East; and therefore to avoid a War, offered them the Choice of this Alternative; either that the *Antients* would please to remove themselves and their effects down to the lower Summity, which the *Moderns* would graciously surrender to them, and advance in their Place; or else that the said *Antients* will give leave to the *Moderns* to come with Shovels and Mattocks, and level the said Hill, as low as they shall think it convenient. To which, the *Antients* made Answer: How little they expected such a Message as this, from a Colony, whom they had admitted out of their own Free Grace, to so near a Neighborhood. That as to their own Seat, they were *Aborigines* of it, and therefore, to talk with them of a Removal or Surrender, was a language they did not understand. That, if the Height of the Hill, on their side, shortened the Prospect of the *Moderns,* it was a Disadvantage they could not help, but desired them to consider, whether that Injury (if it be any) were not largely recompensed by the *Shade* and *Shelter* it afforded them. That, as to the levelling or digging down, it was either Folly or Ignorance to propose it, if they did or did not know, how that side of the Hill was an entire Rock, which would break their Tools and Hearts; without any Damage to itself. That they would therefore advise the *Moderns,* rather to raise their own side of the Hill, than dream of pulling down that of the *Antients,* to the former of which, they would not only give licence, but also largely contribute."

JONATHAN SWIFT

From *The Life and Friendships of Dean Swift,* by STEPHEN GWYNNE

PREFACE

THE history of the arts is the history of the civilization of man; and of all the arts man has produced, painting and sculpture seem to cause the greatest speculation as to the why and wherefore of their existence. Inquiring minds engaged in probing this subject are bringing forth many answers to their questionings, but whether these are clarifying is quite another matter. It would seem, even as we approach the middle of the twentieth century, that the arts still stand beyond the power of man to explain their existence, although they are his own creation.

Therefore the reader may think that art needs no defense. He will be quite right in this, for when we permit art to speak for itself we find it entirely competent to say all that is needed. It is when we do not allow it to speak for itself but listen, instead, to all those who would speak for it, that it has need of defense, for, much as it is to be regretted, it is from its many and sometimes, even, its most devoted spokesmen that it most needs to be defended.

There are many contemporary books by writers on art that are better understood and appraised when examined in the light of the artist's point of view. For much talk that does not follow from practical accomplishment is more likely to mislead than to be constructive.

The task before the thinking reader today is to note as best he can, and in the most objective manner possible, what appears to be taking place about him in the world of art—not merely to read the words in the books he chooses, but to weigh their meaning. In one respect he may find that our world today appears to be behaving true to form, for, without much doubt, it is characteristic of most periods of history that a war should be in progress between the Ancients and the Moderns for supremacy in thinking and in doing. Looking back over the many centuries of the known history of art he will note the great splendor in which the battle of today is being waged in comparison with earlier conflicts—the many forces arrayed in brilliant words which are brought to bear against one another.

In a brief survey of contemporary writing on art this book attempts to show the layman and the student what kind of thought is advanced for their consumption. The survey is necessarily brief and incomplete because the only alternative for the treatment of matters so complex would be a book of great length which very few people would read, even were the author capable of writing it.

Here it would be pertinent to pause for a moment to ask who, in art, are the Ancients and the Moderns? They are said to be, respectively, those who uphold Tradition and those who desire to break with it. But words are deceptive. It is the work of art which has made Tradition, not Tradition the work of art. It is genius which keeps Tradition alive and not Tradition which fosters genius. Possibly, then, the Ancients and the Moderns are not the artists themselves, for art, when we take a bird's-eye view of it, discloses itself to be neither ancient nor modern, but simply Art.

These pages, then, are primarily concerned with those things which, today, are being said about art, and in particular about the art of painting. A term—non-traditional—has been used in referring to those contemporary painters who have sought to break the bonds which they consider Tradition imposes upon the artist, not because they are modern in the sense of belonging to our own time or even because their works differ, to our eyes, from traditional works to which we are accustomed; but because of the kind of thought which, we are told, has impelled them to take their different course. To be modern is in every sense desirable although it is frequently uncomfortable because subject to misinterpretation; and of misinterpretation of non-traditional—or, as they have often been called, modernistic—works what have we not seen in the past four decades! It is worth bearing in mind that it is not necessary to be non-traditional in order to be modern, and it is also worth mentioning at this point that works not displaying representational form may, conceivably, embody the essentials of traditional form. What it is even more necessary to understand is that it is not the mere fact of being modern which is of importance, but how, in what manner, we are modern.

The reader will see for himself that much which applies to one art also applies to the arts in general, if he approaches the subject with a wary spirit not to be caught in the dangers of too-easy generalization. This book, also, in contrast to most books on art, offers the reader no new theories for his consideration. Instead, it suggests that common sense should be used in considering those theories which are so plentifully advanced for the clarification of a subject as vast as it is profound, as involved as it is elusive. And common sense is sorely needed, for today thought about art has reached a state of confusion unequaled in any period of its history.

It has been said that unless, at times, we disregard common sense in order to follow emotional experience we shall make no progress in our way of thought. This may very well be true, but whether it be so or not, if we leave it at that we simply beg the question. As artists, we should apply what common sense we may have to the understanding of our experience, otherwise we shall not be thinking about it but merely talking about it blindly, or for the sake of effect. It is the result of the experience which matters and, for the artist, that result should be realization of his intention, not in words but in his own medium. Without this realization on the part of the artist there can be neither appreciation nor worth-while criticism of the artist's achievement on the part of the observer.

There was a time, happily, when the layman was able to say, without fear of being thought ignorant, that although he knew nothing about art, he knew what he liked. Today, unhappily, all sorts of strange, apparently knowing phrases have come to take the place of this wholesome aphorism; phrases about "textures," "spatial volumes," "plastic form," "rhythm," which sound learned but which frequently confuse the issue and cause him to lose sight of his individual preference. Possibly it is better to know nothing about art and to be able to say whether or not one likes what one sees, than that the mind should be occupied with plausible theories concerning it; theories accepted and discussed as matters of knowledge. For to know something about art requires study of its practice, a fact too readily forgotten in theoretical discussion. Theories have the power to fascinate the imagination and to cast a spell over the thinking mind which obscures the more simple, spontaneous matter of preference when it does not conquer it altogether.

It is said that art, during the past one hundred years or so, has been gradually removed from life and set apart for worship upon a pedestal. The writers say that museums, collectors and dealers are responsible for this unhappy isolation. But few theoretical writers about art seem to realize their own greater responsibility; for it is more often they who obscure the artist's way of thought to the world at large.

That the artist cares comparatively little for theory and much for doing, is too little known. But theorists who write say they know this well; and, having said it, appear content, and return with a free conscience to the manufacture of obscurity.

He who seeks a knowledge of art will do well to close his ears and open his eyes—those much maligned instruments of vision—for through their use he will still find in a bewildered world much to make him wise.

DEFENSE OF ART

CHAPTER ONE

THE CONFUSION OF LANGUAGE

WE who live in this impatient twentieth century have the habit of self-analysis and of appraising all we do while in the act of doing—a habit of mind destructive to creative thought. Of this there is great evidence in our art today. As artists, we are not content to do and let posterity judge of our accomplishment, but must be advertising our special qualifications, our particular claims to superiority over the past, in the most spectacular language and with the greatest show we can contrive. And if our intentions are not apparent in our works books appear at hand, as if by magic, in explanation of their artistic and their "cultural" value.

In the early part of the seventeenth century an Englishman traveling in the East wrote: "The beginnings and progresses of Naturall Philosophy being in this manner, we neede not demande whether the Aegiptians did teach, or were taught for learning has sometimes flourished in a country, and at another time hath bin in exile: . . . It is most likely that in the plantation of the world the worst men were the seekers of new seats, and peradventure the confusion of language was the destruction of arts, and it is certain that the knowledge of arts came from the East where the first plantation was." Much has here been said to give us thought. To say whether learning flourishes with us today, or is in exile, is not our concern, for only posterity will know. But it should be our concern, if we seek a knowledge of the arts—in our reading of books about them—to have some understanding of the kinds of principles and ideas from which they spring and without which they cannot exist. The suggestion made by this thoughtful traveler three hundred years ago that the confusion of language, that is, the confusion of thought expressed in speech or writing was, peradventure, the destruction of arts even in earlier times, applies most emphatically to the speech and writing about art in our own day. Not because the spoken and the written word have destroyed the arts, nor even in the end are likely to do so; but because they possess the power to obscure the sense of what is believed about them. Things said or written often appear fraught with meaning because of the manner of their expression, which upon further examination make little sense or none at all. For writing, as has been said, is an attempt to express thought in words, and thought which purports to analyze the works of others can render, at best, only partial aspects of those works. In his own medium the artist states the whole, whereas it is in the rarest instances only, when the writer is an artist in his own right, that his verbal appraisal of the painter's and the sculptor's art may capture and convey that whole in verbal form.

Aesthetic judgment lends itself too readily to error to be more than partly true, and part-truths carry with them great deceptions. The wonder is not that he who attempts to write about the arts does more to confuse his special purpose than to clarify it, but that he continues to live happily, unaware of what manner of sin he has fallen into. Or perhaps he is not unaware of it but, like the strong man who digests his sin, acknowledges it, and continues on his way regardless of it. For he tells the reader that theories and abstract definitions of art are futile; that the moment definition is attempted it destroys those qualities it seeks to characterize. And, having said this to his satisfaction, he continues to write books about art in which he invents more theories and more definitions. These theories and definitions the student and the layman absorb in eager expectation of learning something about art. It is not astonishing, then, that what we read about art contributes so little to its comprehension.

This is not only true of the arts in general, it is particularly true of painting and sculpture which, because of their complex characters, give unlimited opportunity for indeterminable speculation as to their natures.

The restless desire to understand cause and effect that prevailed in the last two centuries has led eager investigators into every kind of analytical research. Not only artists and writers, but the amateur artistic and literary circles all did a great deal of talking, speculating, theorizing, and writing about art. Most prominent among these earnest thinkers were the philosophers, historians, essayists; and last, but not least, the critics. Today their ranks have been swelled by the psychologists and psychoanalysts, and the general writer on art who is none of these specialists in his own right but has caught their many ways of thought and styles himself an aesthetician. Building upon one another's theories, all have taken advantage of the opportunity to explain, and to exploit unchecked, as their imaginations see fit, the mysteries of artistic creation about which little or nothing is known.

Unfortunately for him, the artist appears to be someone whose very being arouses the curiosity of his fellows. They must speculate as to the mysteries of his way of life and the reasons for his singular desire to make images on a flat surface with colors, or to mold them in solid materials. And usually the result of such speculations is to endow him with motives and ideas which have never entered his consciousness; with thoughts and desires too remote from his mind to be real to him, and which, when he is made aware of them in the books he reads, or in conversation, come to him as a painful surprise. There is a great discrepancy between the artist's way of thinking and the kind of thought attributed to him in critical appreciation of his works. Problems relative to the production of works of art are sufficient to engross his entire attention without the irrelevant thought contributed by the literary point of view. All art is to him primarily art and the product of a creative imagination. But the writer on art appears no longer to consider art as art, being intent upon classifying the different styles and kinds of works produced by man since the beginning of the world, according to whatsoever theories he can devise within which to fit a comprehensive system of analytical appreciation. To the artist, on the other hand, there is good art and false art, and art which is superlative; whether this be ancient or modern is, for the most part, immaterial. He regards the different modes of presentation as so many different manifestations of the same kind of thought. Cults and sects given over to the pursuit of theory are of little importance to him, and in some cases of no importance at all; nor does he spend his thought and energy devising ways of reacting from or revolting against accepted methods. Edouard Manet speaks of this in the foreword which he wrote to the catalogue of an exhibition he was to hold at a time when his works were bitterly disliked and criticized. He says: "The effect of sincerity is to give to works a character that makes them resemble a protest, when the only concern of a painter has been to render his impression. M. Manet has never wished to protest. On the contrary, the protest, quite unexpected on his part, has been directed against himself because there exists a traditional teaching as to forms, methods, modes of painting, and because those who have been brought up in this tradition refuse to admit any other. . . . M. Manet . . . has had no pretensions either to overthrow an established mode of painting, or to create a new one. He has simply tried to be himself and not another."

But in books on art the artist is pictured as a rebel in revolt against the standards of his day, seeking to destroy what is, and to replace it with something else; if possible, with something new. Evolution does not proceed in this manner nor does creation prosper where the mind is bent upon revolt. Constructive work is not done in a destructive spirit; a work undertaken in the spirit of antagonism or of hate is unlikely to become a work of art. Nevertheless, we have the unfortunate habit of speaking of new ways of thought as being "revolutionary." The word, in relation to the arts, is misleading and arouses confusion and misconception. So great are these, indeed, that many people believe the spirit of revolt is a necessity to artistic creation. And not merely a blind desire to revolt against existing forms of art, but that emotions aroused by the spectacle of human suffering and the need for social reform are vital to creative energy. This subject would require a book to itself, but here it must suffice to say that whatever the source of the artist's thought and feeling—and we may be sure that its nature is highly complex—when he undertakes the presentation of his idea it is the picture he is about to make, and the way he chooses to make it, which absorb his entire being. Creation begins when the spirit of antagonism has lost its fire and the force which is love of the work in progress toward the desired conclusion comes to take its place. The artist who turns aside from the prevailing modes and methods of procedure taught in the schools of his day, does so because he finds them inadequate to his purpose, not because his spirit is in revolt against them.

Breasted, in *Ancient Times*,* makes this very clear when he speaks of the way earliest man went about the making of his implements. "He noticed that his stone, as furnished ready made by nature, was not well

* Permission of the publishers, Ginn and Company.

suited to his purpose; that is, he inspected its shape and ventured to disapprove of it. Disapproval is a very important factor in all progress. There has really never been any progress without it. Striking his native rock fragment upon another stone, some primitive man with more initiative than his fellows endeavored to improve the shape of the pebble he had picked up, and to suit its shape to the use for which he needed it." In disapproval of that which is inadequate to his purpose and in his endeavor to mold the means at his disposal toward a realization of the end he has in view, we find the spirit in which an artist works.

But the authors of books on art have long since forgotten the main issue, and the artist's attitude, like the forest that could not be seen for the trees, has been lost to view in an overgrowth of theories. And these theories, grown wild as weeds, have become unrealities which cannot be considered in terms of art.

Since the turn of the twentieth century the novel problems presented in the works of contemporary artists who fear being held in bondage by tradition have greatly increased the complexity of the entire subject. But this has in no way deterred the writers on art. They have, on the contrary, served the cause of confusion by their encouragement of extravagant thinking.

Despite the confusion and obscurity which their

writing produces, two threads of thought become apparent throughout its course. One is an attempt to point out the fundamental difference between that art which, prior to the twentieth century, made and kept tradition alive, and the non-traditional art of our day; the other is an attempt to show how this last may be considered the natural sequel to the art of the past.

The following chapters undertake to show the layman and the student the "confusion of language" in which these thoughts are set forth.

___

CHAPTER TWO

THIS ACADEMIC TRADITION

THE public is asked to consider certain theories as illuminating to artistic problems, both past and present. Therefore we shall begin our examination into these theories with what their authors have to say about the art of the past, for there we find the foundation for what they say of the art of our own time.

The quotations from their writings have been chosen, not because they speak the thought of any one writer, or because such writings are works of distinction, but rather because of the kind of thought they exemplify— a kind of thought in which confusion is often the worse confounded because of the undeniable elements of truth it also presents.

The following extract is from a book by Herbert Read called *Art Now*, from the chapter on the Academic Tradition, "What the Eye Sees": "The main tradition of European painting, that tradition which for convenience I shall call *academic*, begins in the fourteenth century. Without attaching too much importance to any individual, like Giotto, we may say without much fear of contradiction that it begins with the desire to reproduce in some way exactly what the eye sees."

Now the significance of tradition in painting and sculpture becomes obscured by the constant reiteration in art criticism today of this particular interpretation of it. When we speak of a work as academic, or belonging to the academic tradition, we are apt to apply the term in a derogatory sense: meaning that it is limited in conception, that its execution is circumscribed by convention and rule, that the effect of the whole is what writers call photographic. Mr. Read also says: "The traditional art of the Renaissance, the art of Humanism, in spite of all its periodical changes, remains one tradition right down to the Impressionist and even to the Post Impressionist schools. That tradition, now crystallized as contemporary academic art, remains constant and uncontaminated; and however much we may rail against it, it does not die, and judging by the popular and official support given it, it does not even decay."

In the light of these comments it would be interesting to consider the true significance of the "academic tradition," for the persistence of its standard in the arts appears to occasion these writers surprise, if not irritation and dismay. There may be some explanation for a tradition which has remained for so long constant and uncontaminated, which does not die, or even decay.

As is well known, tradition in the art of painting means the knowledge of procedure handed down from generation to generation from those already skilled in their art to their pupils. That knowledge has its root in the days when early man began to adorn his implements, his dwelling and himself; to communicate with his fellows by the natural means of graphic forms whose shapes were recognizable; a knowledge that has been added to over hundreds of thousands of years down to our own day. But this is not all tradition means today. It means also a knowledge and understanding of past achievement—of what man has been able to do with the materials at his disposal, as well as how he has done it. From a late civilization in Greece, from the garden of one Academus, where Plato and many another Greek philosopher taught, we take the name, academy, which means, simply, a place of learning. To the civilized world the academic tradition in the art of painting signifies that through the artist's sense of sight, thought and emotion, the knowledge and wisdom of the human race have been re-presented to the observer's senses within the precincts of visual art. There is always a contemporary art in which knowledge of procedure becomes crystallized in the popular method of the day by those whose gifts do not rise to great expression. We forget that "academic" works such as these also serve a purpose however much we may "rail" against them. They are often works of great merit and of beauty but in them the significance of traditional form remains stationary in acknowledgment of past and of contemporary achievement. These works form a background against which we may see, and with which we may compare, those works of genius in which tradition is a vital force; a force which does not decay but which creates, instead, the stepping stones of evolution.

We return to the first statement quoted from Mr. Read's book, because for all its seeming clarity he makes in it the most dangerous of all pronouncements, the part-truth; the part-truth upon which theories of art find such easy nourishment. We may undoubtedly accept the idea that fourteenth-century European painters desired to present in some way as nearly as possible what the eye saw; but so also did the painters and the sculptors of Greece, the painters and sculptors of Egypt, and the earlier artists who drew and painted upon rock in caves. The learning of the fourteenth century in Europe is also the learning of these earlier peoples. To judge from their works we may assume that artists in these widely separated times were not only occupied in presenting, in recognizable form, what they had seen but also what they thought and felt about what they saw. Mr. Read fails to allow for these additional factors. He also fails to allow for the most important point of all, that what the spectator sees in these artists' works is what they *made* of what they thought and felt through the medium of their sight.

The theory that the traditional artist's desire is to reproduce exactly what the eye sees is a favorite one in current literature on art. But to reproduce exactly is to copy, and the works of nature, while they may be imitated, cannot be copied or reproduced. Nor is the artist interested in reproducing anything—he gives his greatest efforts to the presentation of something. There is no question of exactitude; he does the best he can to make a vital image of that which he has conceived. His work lies in the correlation of those things which he is predisposed to see in nature—in bringing diversity to a homogeneous conclusion. Matters of art are primarily matters of relationship, not of accuracy or of exactness in the artist's way of seeing. Accuracy and exactness necessarily imply that the same thing shall be seen in the same way by all who see it, without variation. They imply what is impossible in the art of painting where original work is concerned; impossible because of the composition of the human being, because of the elements of which nature is composed, and because of the character and limitations of the artist's materials.

Leonardo da Vinci said, at the height of that period which causes the writer of today such mental anguish, the Renaissance: "You should apply yourself first of all to drawing in order to present to the eye, in visible form, the purpose and invention created originally in your imagination." In view of this statement by an artist of the Renaissance, and of what we learn from history, it becomes increasingly difficult to find the academic tradition beginning with the desire to reproduce exactly what the eye sees in the fourteenth century A.D. And yet our contemporary writers on art are attempting to develop a comprehensive system of artistic appreciation based on this theory.

The English traveler said: ". . . It is certain that the knowledge of arts came from the East where the first plantation was," and it is also certain that the earliest records of analytical thought on artistic matters came from Greece, the link between the East and the West. Although records of Greek thought on art are few and far between, they show great preoccupation with the idea of imitation; an idea which has persisted throughout the centuries down to our own time. It is an important idea and we should see what has been made of it.

Plato said the artist imitated appearances, and that

his works could easily be made without any knowledge of the truth; and he implied that because of these things his product was of an inferior order. Jowett says that "Plato was not lost in rapture at the great works of Phidias, the Parthenon, the Propylea, the statues of Zeus or Athene. He would probably have regarded any abstract truth of number or of figure as higher than the greatest of them. . . . Whether or no, like some writers, he felt more than he expressed, it is at any rate remarkable that the greatest perfection of the fine arts should coincide with an almost entire silence about them."

But Plato's Socrates, in his wisdom and humor, was not consistent in his condemnation of the arts as inferior, or as serving no good purpose in the cultivation of virtue. For he also calls them a kind of creation and says of the painter, as of the poet, that such a man may keep his thoughts in his mind for a considerable time after they have occurred to him, and that at such times his soul is like a book where memory and perception meet. He then draws images in the soul of things he has seen and heard described. And the images answering to true opinions and words are true, and to false opinions and words false. Socrates also goes so far as to say that in giving due proportion to the features of a work we make the whole beautiful.

After Plato comes Aristotle, to whom imitation signified the presentation of whatever the artist had imagined which could be perceived by the senses. To him soul and body were the inner and the outer aspects of the same object, so that the inner meaning of a thing is vitally connected with its outer manifestation. After Aristotle we take a long stride and cover many centuries, from the time Greek civilization was at its height to the rebirth of learning in Europe. Much that was known to the Greeks was lost to later civilizations through the destruction of their works, so that Renaissance artists knew but little of their achievements. This is particularly the case with the works of Greek painters. But throughout the long, quiescent period of the Dark Ages, which we are beginning to see was, perhaps, not quite so dark as we have been given to believe, something of their knowledge was kept alive by Roman interest in the arts, though of opinion about them there appears to be little recorded. Nevertheless tradition was fostered for ten or more centuries of the Christian era, and when the art of painting was reborn in Europe it was from the knowledge which came from the East that artists again learned their procedure, and from the remains of Eastern works that they learned of man's achievement in art.

We learn, then, from what we read that ideas of

imitation are well established in the minds of men since the days of the Greeks, and for the most natural reasons. There are two senses in which we think of imitation in relation to painting and sculpture. The least significant but most generally understood results from the artist's use of images of familiar forms in the making of his works--the instinctive means of visual expression. Imitation in this sense is limited and implies that the artist's aim is the representation of objects. The larger view, in general much less well understood, is expressive of a fundamental, intuitive process realized by creative minds of all kinds because it is the natural mode of approach to their subject. In this sense of imitation, to use Leonardo's words, the artist presents to the eye in visible form the purpose and invention originally created in his imagination. In their application to the creative arts the two meanings are one and cannot be separated because they represent a continuous and inevitable thought process.

To enforce his stand and for the satisfactory development of his thesis Mr. Read, in *Art Now*, quotes the eminent critic, Roger Fry, writing on the same subject. Fry says: "It was required of the artist not only that his imagery should appeal to the emotions by its rhythm, but that it should conform to the appearance of the actual world. Its texture had to be as continuous and unbroken as that of the visible scene. That continuity of texture might be obtained in two ways, either by accurate imitation of an actual scene or by constructing a picture according to those optical laws to which our vision inevitably conforms. The former, the empirical method, was used in northern Europe by Flemish artists, the latter, the scientific, was worked out in Italy, especially by the Florentines, who first discovered the optical laws of appearance."

These statements are mystifying, the more so as they appear to be made as statements of fact. Empirical Flemish or scientific Italian, a comparison of these early Renaissance painters' works shows them to be equally empirical and equally scientific, if, indeed, they can be said to be either. Possibly Italian artists were acquainted with the sciences of anatomy and perspective earlier in their history than were the Flemish, but of this we have no certain knowledge. On the other hand, the Flemish painters were considered to be greatly in advance of the rest of Europe in their knowledge of oil painting and their skill in its use. Moreover, artists traveled in these times and pupils were sent forth to learn throughout the countries of Europe, and knowledge of one another's methods was not long in spreading.

When we speak of continuity of texture in a work of art we refer to a quality of its technique. With this particular quality the optical laws of appearance have nothing to do. Pictures may be constructed according to such laws with rough and broken textures, as are those of many painters of the late nineteenth century, and as are the great majority of pictures today. Nor do the textures of pictures necessarily bear any resemblance to the textures of the visible scene. We have only to compare mountains, trees, rocks, buildings, the human body, with the textures of paint on canvas, or on wood or plaster, in any work of art, rough or smooth. To obtain continuity of texture by constructing pictures according to the optical laws of appearance is as improbable a method of obtaining any kind of texture as the "accurate imitation of an actual scene" is impracticable.

It is evident from what we read that the mental processes of the Greek thinkers were clearer and more profound, and their opinions on matters of art truer, than are those of our contemporary writers whose thinking may be said to be neither clear nor profound. They were also, we venture to suggest, of a truer order than those of our European thinkers of the Middle Ages and the eighteenth and nineteenth centuries, for it is to these great philosophers that we owe much of the confused thought of our day—a kind of thought which would not have been possible to those in search of knowledge in the fifth century B.C.

To conclude his chapter on the academic tradition,

and to bring the popular theory of a mechanistic art to its full development, Herbert Read says: "Here, already, within a description of the academic tradition, we have two methods indicated, the *empirical* and the *scientific*, and these two terms will describe the content of contemporary academic art. As its name implies, the empirical method succeeds, by whatever technical deftness it can devise, in giving an illusion of direct, visual experience. It is the imitative method in all its naïveté, and just because it is imitative, and has no other aim than the reproduction of appearances, it is of little theoretical interest. You may be satisfied with this type of art; you may demand of the artist an exact record of the record given by the physiological mechanism of his sight. If so, all that you can demand of the artist is in its essence mechanical. He must be a perfect machine. The rest is in the subject painted, and about that we may have our opinions, our sentiments, even our emotions; but they have nothing to do with the working of the machine. Thus the empirical method in painting, like the same method in philosophy, ends in materialism: it is a mechanistic theory of art."

Would that conclusions might always be thus simply and satisfactorily reached!

But let us consider for a moment the artist's procedure. After a certain stage in his development, be he of the fourteenth century or of the twentieth, and after a certain skill which comes of practice, technical deftness becomes an exemplification of his individual way of seeing, thinking and feeling; it becomes significant of quality of mind, for the tool can only achieve as the mind conceives. And quality of mind means the functioning of intellect moved by spirit, two parts of man's being working together in harmony. The artist's ability to express his desire in the medium of his choice is commensurate with these qualities of his gift, and the creation of something called a work of art implies them in its creator.

Technical deftness such as that of the Flemish and Italian painters came of a profound understanding, inherent in their genius, of the problems concerning their art. Their gifts, combined with the acquired knowledge which came from observation and study of the essential character of form and color, gave the world certain of its greatest works of art. That these painters studied with deliberate intention, to know and understand to the utmost of their ability what they saw before them, we can scarcely doubt. But the authors of theory appear to forget that such "actual scenes" as they painted must have been composed by the artists themselves. The elaborate paintings involving many figures, landscape and architecture, on both small and large scales, could not have been done from scenes actually before them, scenes which could be "accurately imitated." It was because they studied their materials so closely that they were able to use freely, creatively, the knowledge they acquired by their observations, and that they were then able to give expression to their ideas.

Imitative painting achieved by technical deftness and scientific knowledge is not a creative art. The imitative artist adopts the manner of another and does little or no thinking for himself. Of such there are always many, at all times, but it is not of them that we speak here. No artist who expends sincerely his greatest efforts to render what *he sees* in nature is an imitator. However little gifted he may be, he recreates, to some degree, that which, as an individual, he perceives; for it is only by means of such individual vision which combines seeing, feeling and thinking that he can, through observation, take anything at all from nature. And that which he observes is always stamped with the mark of the limit of his understanding; that which he creates of what he takes is the measure of his stature as an artist.

In the outward manifestations of nature, in her shapes as we see them, is to be found the key to those principles of form which lie beneath the surface and according to which her growth, animal or vegetable, is distributed. They are indices to its character: and it is to the genius of the creative artist who recognizes those qualities through all the accidentals and irregularities of the outer manifestation, who has the power to incorporate them and make them a part of his conception, that the world owes the great works of art of all periods of history. It is the artist who is able to use knowledge of every kind, to mold it to serve his ends, who gives the world new works, and in so doing makes tradition a living force, the force which holds the life-germ of arts as yet unborn.

As we have seen the mechanistic theory of art developed and concluded, so we shall also see the equally popular scientific theory brought to conclusion by Herbert Read. He says: "Once Constable had shown that the colours in a painting could be fresh and vivid as the colours in nature, the artist was set on a new scientific trend, which ended in the scientific, or pseudo-scientific colour schemes of the Pointillists like Seurat and Signac. I say 'ended' there, because for once science was applied too severely to art, and it was realized that analysis pushed too far ends by destroying the very aim of the scientific method in art, which is still to reproduce the appearance of the actual world. 'Continuity of texture' was no longer obtained by this means, and the scientific method itself became doubtful in principle."

On the authority of Herbert Read and Roger Fry

we have mechanistic and scientific theories of art, whose aim is the reproduction, in some way, of the appearance of the actual world. It is worthy of note that while artists have always searched eagerly for knowledge, the invention of such theories as these has been left to the ingenious minds of writers on art. From them we learn that science, that is, the pursuit of knowledge, is responsible for thwarting, or limiting, artistic expression. But science and the arts have held their respective places in the world throughout many centuries and each is too firmly rooted in its own order to be dominated by the other. Although achievement in each field is the result of the same sort of mental attitude—an objective absorption in the matter in hand—there lies a great gulf between the ends each is designed to fulfill; the one with the kind of idea that leads to uncovering truth, the other with the kind of idea which produces an appearance of truth. In the first the idea must be resolvable into fact, or it is valueless as an idea; in the second, the process is reversed: concrete form must comply with the idea or the work is meaningless as a work of art. Neither in the time of the Renaissance in Europe, nor at other times in the history of art when scientific discoveries have been made, has the knowledge derived from them thwarted the expression of the artist who is first a creator. Science has served to increase technical knowledge but not artistic knowledge. Scientific knowledge is a different learning from the knowledge necessary to the art of painting. Science may be of use to art, but only when the two kinds of knowledge are not confused.

Vasari writes that Paolo Uccello "would have been the most gracious and fanciful genius that was ever devoted to the art of painting, from Giotto's day to our own, if he had labored as much at figures and animals as he labored and lost time over the details of perspective; for although these are ingenious and beautiful, yet if a man pursues them beyond measure he does nothing but waste his time, exhaust his powers, fill his mind with difficulties, and often transforms its fertility and readiness into sterility and constraint . . ." And yet was not Uccello's genius of the most gracious and fanciful order in spite of his obsession with the problems of perspective? Few painters have designed so well as he, few have appealed so surely to the emotions by the rhythm of his compositions, to use the phraseology of today. That appeal could not have made itself felt as it did, and as it still does, had his artistic judgment not surpassed even his knowledge and skill in the use of perspective—had he used his gifts only, as Berenson says, "to illustrate scientific problems." This eminent writer, in *Florentine Painters of the Renaissance*, says that Uccello "composed pictures in which he contrived to get as many lines as possible leading the eye inward. Prostrate horses, dead or dying cavaliers, broken lances, ploughed fields, Noah's arks, are used by him with scarcely an attempt at disguise, to serve his theme of mathematically converging lines. In his zeal he forgot local colour—he loved to paint his horses green or pink—forgot action, forgot composition, and, it need scarcely be added, significance." But if Uccello did truly forget all these things, how is it that his works remain, throughout many centuries, among the noted works of the Renaissance? Let us pause for a moment in the midst of words to let some one of this painter's works speak for itself, inasmuch as the immediate result of such writings as these by Berenson, Fry and Read is to fill our minds with irrelevant matter and to cause us to speculate about "mechanistic" and "scientific" theories of art, about "continuity of texture" and "local color," without ever considering the artist's work as a picture. In Uccello's "Battle of S. Egidio" in the National Gallery in London, for instance, the observer, if left to himself, can scarcely fail to be impressed immediately by the spirited design and naïve charm of the presented scene. The "stuffed" horses, the broken lances, the prostrate body of a warrior in fine perspective all take their places as integral parts of the whole work without obtruding themselves in any way. In consequence these characteristic details only enhance the picture's effect as a whole, as a highly wrought work, a presentation significant of a fine imagination. Such an artist as Uccello does not confuse the different aims of science and art. Knowledge is to him no deterrent but, on the contrary, is an inspiration. But because of Uccello's absorption in perspective writers on art must needs confuse the issue in writing of his works. The aims of science and art are all too often confused in this way by the outsider who uses terminologies the practical meaning of which he does not really understand, and which in consequence he greatly exaggerates, confounding all sense. Thus it is that theories of mechanistic and scientific method in art are evolved from without and, in the case of the Renaissance painters, a long time after the painting of their pictures.

Instead of listening to the words of theorists let us turn to the words of Albrecht Dürer who, born in 1471, was not only a great painter but also a goldsmith, a designer and engraver, and, in the later years of his life, spent much time upon problems of geometry, perspective, the proportions of the human figure, and the fortification of towns and castles. He said: "I know not what beauty is; in truth art resides in nature; whoever can draw-it-out therefrom possesses it. The more the aspect of his work conforms to life the better it will be. Therefore do not imagine that you can make something that will improve upon what God has created. By himself, man cannot make a beautiful picture, but, having studied his subject until he is steeped in it, the art thus sown will germinate and bear fruit, and all the secret treasure of the heart will manifest itself in a work that is a new creation."

CHAPTER THREE

THEORIES AND IDEAS

MANY contemporary writers, then, place the significance of traditional form within the limits of mechanistic and scientific theories of art which, they hold, were pushed to their extremes and downfall by painters of the late nineteenth century; and, more particularly, they hold that their breakdown is apparent in the works of the Impressionists.

Thinking in this way, such writers seem to feel justified in asserting that the alleged breakdown of these theories means the breakdown of tradition; that there is no further possibility for artistic development within its bounds. Therefore, they say twentieth-century artists necessarily sought new forms of expression, new modes of thought, which would release them from the fetters of tradition. Artists and writers alike maintain that in the non-traditional works of the twentieth century the disappearance of recognizable form, which accompanied a desire for novelty, is indicative of a deeper search for the essential character of form. These are the things of which we hear. But what of those which we *see?*

One hundred and fifty years ago—toward the end of the eighteenth century—Sir Joshua Reynolds said, in the seventh of his famous Discourses: "It has been the fate of the arts to be enveloped in mysterious and incomprehensible language . . ." and that: "It is necessary that at some time or other we should see things as they really are and not impose on ourselves by that false magnitude with which objects appear when viewed indistinctly as through a mist."

In the time of Sir Joshua the arts were still comprehensible to sight in spite of "mysterious and incomprehensible language" about them, and they continued to be so through to the end of the nineteenth century. But after the Impressionists, through Cézanne, past Van Gogh and Gauguin, the art of painting itself rapidly approached a period of confusion resulting in much that is "mysterious and incomprehensible" to the eye. Thus, today, we have unintelligibility not only in what is said about the arts but actually in a large proportion of the works of painters and sculptors.

It is difficult to trace the seed from which disorder grows, to find just where deterioration of form, in the arts, begins. But wherever the inception may be found it would seem that as men grow more self-conscious they become less creative—as they seek guidance to the solution of their problems by means of theory their works become less vital.

In the works of certain of the Impressionist painters there is a suggestion of dissociation between form and idea; in the first decade of the twentieth century form and idea were severed entirely by artists in search of theories from which to devise a new art.

But newness in art is not so devised. It comes primarily by way of the artist's genius. Fundamental principles in the arts are few and simple, but the variety with which they may be expressed and to which they give rise is infinite and complex. They are always open to new interpretation provided new interpretation is not intentionally sought. Precisely here, in the search for new expression, aesthetic theory obtrudes itself into the artist's realm. When the artist is guided by its teaching his purpose and procedure are all too often confused—an indication that his creative powers are uncertain. For theories are not ideas and cannot serve him in their stead. Their part in the creation of works of art is little understood, their importance greatly exaggerated. The final test of a work of art is the homogeneous presentation of ideas, not the attempt to realize theories.

Ideas are conceptions of the mind, created none knows how. Theories, on the other hand, are contrivances of the mind, hypothetical in nature, designed to assist in the analysis and elucidation of ideas. Theories in the visual arts are of two kinds: one kind seeks to deal with those parts of the whole conception which concern the intangible, or as they are called, the abstract qualities of mind and spirit, which, because of their nature are, in themselves, indefinable in the artist's medium and therefore cannot be rendered consciously in concrete form; the other kind seeks to deal with those parts of the whole which concern the material substance of a work, its method and execution, and may be rendered in concrete form. The artist's method and execution incorporate automatically *and in accordance with his sensibilities* those qualities which are abstract and give them an effect of reality. Thus a work of art becomes the product of the artist's imagination—of his emotional and intellectual experience combined; a visual realization of his idea.

Ruskin, in the *Stones of Venice*, says: "What we want art to do for us is to stay what is fleeting, and to enlighten what is incomprehensible, to incorporate the things that have no measure, and immortalize the things that have no duration and all that . . . in the great natural world is infinite and wonderful, having in it that spirit and power which man may witness, but not weigh; conceive, but not comprehend; love, but

not limit, and imagine, but not define; this, the beginning and the end of all noble art."

And the difficulty is that all these qualities must
make their primary appeal through the sense of sight.
In painting and sculpture this can only be done by
the ordered disposition of recognizable form, whatever the means of its presentation. Art is not achieved
without order, the only foundation of beauty and the
only convincing means of conveying an effect of
reality, an appearance of truth. Whatever abstract
qualities the artist conveys are so conveyed, for form
and idea are then homogeneous. Where form is lacking, bewilderment and uncertainty creep in only to
serve confusion, and to end in nothingness. When we
are unable to recognize form with our eyes we seek
elucidation of the artist's intention in verbal expression; that is, we theorize about what we think he has
tried to do, or what he himself says he has tried to
do.

We have seen the position to which our contemporary writers have assigned the academic tradition,
alleging that it has fulfilled its destiny in the works of
the Impressionist painters; that a mechanistic theory
of art, complicated by scientific knowledge—or pseudo-
scientific, it appears to make little difference which—
can go no further than these works have carried it.
Before we study the literature which tells us the

reasons for this situation we may review the already well-known story of the Impressionist painters, to see what sort of artists they were and what it was they achieved, for they are, perhaps, the most written-about of all nineteenth-century painters prior to Cézanne. Their works have been "enveloped in mysterious and incomprehensible language"—in mists of aesthetic appreciation. These it would be desirable to dispel, for the Impressionists were, first and foremost, artists whose attitude of mind was creative; to whom theory was secondary.

In Paris, in the 1870's, a group of young men were interested in painting from nature, out of doors. They used to meet at the Café Guerbois to discuss their ideas and possible ways and means of rendering effects of light and color. Manet, whom they often met on these occasions, was their great friend and it is said that his way of thinking often inspired theirs, for it was to him that they submitted their problems for advice. When in 1874 they held their first exhibition, their works were received with scorn and derision. Among them was a picture by the young Claude Monet, called "Impression—Soleil Levant," a view in a harbor with boats appearing through the reddish mists of a rising sun. Theodore Duret says: "The exhibition brought the exponents of the new painting in particular into great but disastrous notoriety. The pictures were pronounced to be formless, the artists perverted, ignorant, presumptuous. The exhibition led to one result, however, which they had never anticipated. It gave them something which until then they had lacked—a name." Monet's canvas was particularly characteristic and the title in keeping with its style of execution—"the light rapid touch and general indefiniteness of the outlines. Such a work adequately expressed the formula of the new painting. Thus, by its title and its technique, it suggested the term which appeared most aptly to characterize the artists belonging to the new school—that of Impressionists." This name was used for a long time in a derogatory sense by their critics, but many of the painters—not all, for some protested against it—felt that it was justified, that they were attempting to render their impressions, as Manet had said of himself some years before in the foreword to his catalogue; and they finally decided, after several years had elapsed, to adopt it themselves. They had a long struggle for material success which was not rewarded until the 1890's when their works attracted buyers both at home and abroad.

Manet and Degas are usually considered Impressionists. But this is only so in that they were interested in similar problems. They were older men and, though intimate friends, were not, as painters, of the group of Impressionists proper. Their forms of expression were of a very different character. Manet did not exhibit in company with the Impressionists, and it is said that Degas did so only out of friendship. Of the immediate circle of Impressionists Pissarro, Monet, Sisley and Renoir are the outstanding figures today. All were simple and objective in their way of thinking. They believed that certain colors carefully juxtaposed would render more truly the effects in nature which they thought beautiful than any method hitherto employed. Their technique and the theories of scientific color mixture on which it is said to have been based were second in importance to their desire to present works consistent in their effect. As to the science of their theories there is considerable confusion. Because they were guided in a general way by certain facts about light and color it does not mean that the Impressionists painted scientifically, or even that their attitude of mind was scientific. It is one thing to be guided by scientific fact in the development of a technique of oil painting, and quite another to be accurate in the use of such fact. The Impressionists were in no sense accurate in the use of their knowledge, and where there is no accuracy in the application of theory and method, neither is there true science. The Impressionists' color theories were entirely at the mercy of their individual judgments as artists. The marked differences of character in their works are sufficient to show that this is so. As to their technique generally speaking, when certain colors are set side by side upon canvas they make an impression of greater brilliance to the eye (because, at a little distance, the mixture is achieved in optical effect) than when colors are mixed beforehand on the palette, when the new mixture thus formed appears comparatively dull. Doubtless the Impressionists' technique and their handling of color contributed much toward a clearer, fresher use of pigments than had been obtained for many years in the methods of painting taught in the schools. If these painters' works do not stand in the first rank of artistic achievement it was not science that hindered a greater fulfillment but the quality of their genius which was not equal to greater heights of accomplishment. As with Uccello and perspective, so with the Impressionists and theories of color-mixture, it is essential to distinguish between what, through science, they learned of the aspects of nature, and what, as artists, they considered fit for employment in their works. Far more important than their "science" and first in the consciousness of these painters were their individual ideas as to what they wanted to present. Scientific knowledge is of little use to the artist unless he has the power to make it subservient to his artistic judgment.

The Impressionists did not set out to be Impressionists in a spirit of revolt against the methods of painting taught in their day, nor to found a school by that name. They did not bind themselves to the pursuit of theory for its own sake, nor did they attempt to do new things for the sake of novelty. They were, simply, painters who devised a technique which they considered would suit their ends.

It can only be guessed how the extravagant theorizings of writers on art have been aided by what had been heard of the conversations in the Café Guerbois. These writers forget that however brilliantly a painter may talk he, too, is human in his enthusiasms, but that if he is to paint he must occupy himself with the matter in hand to the exclusion of all but his ultimate purpose. Because the writers forget these things the most astounding misconceptions of artistic procedure remain current in the world.

Let us see what Thomas Craven, in his book, *Modern Art*, says of these painters. "Impressionism carried on the healthy realism of Courbet and Manet by dispensing with conventional subject matter, drew attention to the artistic material in the nooks and corners of the everyday world, eliminated quantities of ugly mud from the palette, and codified the relation of light-values to color." All this is excellent, although we might take issue with the verifiability of the last-mentioned item. But then Mr. Craven astounds us by saying: "All this had the defect of leaving the mind unemployed." But, we might ask, whose mind? And, after reading his chapter, suggest that it was Mr. Craven's. It would be difficult to imagine the minds of the Impressionists wandering at leisure in all the nooks and corners of the earth while their bodies, energetically employed before their easels, painted "nature exactly as seen"—a "jolly outdoor sport."

Another writer, Mary Cecil Allen, in *Painters of the Modern Mind*, disarms us by saying: "And in order to judge a drawing or a painting, it is necessary to refrain from adding anything to it in our minds; from helping the artist out, as it were. We must inhibit such mental action and coldly receive just as much as the picture is able to convey. This is the first condition of art appreciation. There must be no appreciatory attitude of mind." There could be no more admirable statement than this, but its value is entirely undone by the pages which follow, offering the unwary reader material with which to form an appreciatory attitude of mind. As we read, we re-arm, for we are told that "Impressionism took the physical eye as the sole standard of reference . . ." It was, "in short, a magnificent technical method based upon the seeing power of the eye rather than on any evaluation of the thing seen."

But, as we have said before, if not quite in the same words, in the art of painting the seeing power of the eye is inseparable from the mind's "evaluation" of the thing seen. The Impressionist technique was based upon the keenest sort of evaluation of the thing seen. As a method of painting it is the reverse of magnificent, for it is perhaps the most unwieldy that has ever been invented. It is slow, and requires detailed thought at the same time that it must accomplish a consistent whole, a completed unit, with the utmost speed. The painter must analyze his subject; he must have a memory so keen and sensitive that it may retain the first impression after its analysis, that it may aid him to bring the whole to a conclusion. And this is a difficult thing to do while carefully selecting and placing little spots of color on areas of canvas as large as those the Impressionists were prone to use. In the use of this method the painter's mind is, indeed, occupied with so many questions at one time that only the gifted artist avoids confusion. But such were Monet's and Pissarro's gifts that they succeeded in bringing certain paintings to life as works of art.

Reading further in Miss Allen's book we are told that "Painters were haunted by the thought of absolute truth." But what, we may ask, is the absolute truth of light and color where the art of painting is under consideration? In January of the year 1672, Sir

Isaac Newton wrote to the secretary of the Royal Society, of which institution he had lately been elected a member, saying that he purposed the Society to consider and examine "an account of a philosophical discovery . . . being in my judgment the oddest if not the most considerable detection which hath hitherto been made into the operations of nature." It was thus that he referred to his discovery of the composition of white light, or, let us say, his discovery of an absolute truth. Now the Impressionists knew something of these things, but no matter how deeply their thoughts may have been engaged with a knowledge of facts, they knew that an artist's concern is not absolute truth, but relative truth—the presentation of an appearance of truth. Nor were they the first to be fascinated by speculation as to the "operations" of nature. Leonardo, a tireless student of natural phenomena, a man far ahead of his time, observed and made note of many things. He was aware of the very problems to which the Impressionists addressed themselves, and he predicted with wisdom that a preoccupation with effects of light and color in nature is likely to result in the confusion of form. That form was of less interest to the Impressionists than color-effect is evident in their works.

At this point we place before the reader a matter for his consideration: that seldom, perhaps never, in the history of painting have form and color—or, let us say, form and color-effect—appeared with equal force in the works of any one painter. We refer to realized works, not to the sketch or study, in which both are frequently suggested with equal conviction. Yet it is necessary to remember what is all too often overlooked, that, owing to the composition of pigments and the vehicles with which they are applied, color seldom survives for long with its original freshness and brilliance. Modern research into the history of painting, the documents descriptive of materials and the methods of their use, as well as the state of some paintings preserved to us from early times, indicate that colors were as brilliant when first applied in days long past as are colors in our day. These things must be taken into account in observing the works of masters of form of the past, both near and far, for in the majority of cases we, today, can only guess what their original color-effect may have been.

On the other hand, even if a preoccupation with problems of light and color is likely to confuse the form—as it doubtless will in the works of all but the greatest—artists will, nevertheless, continue to study those problems. And, in some more fortunate time than ours, when all that has been written about Impressionism is forgotten; when the foolish grinning specters raised by writers on art no longer confront an artist whichever way he turns, to confuse the issue and, if possible, to confound his thought, we may look for works resulting from such study which will be new and impartial presentations of form and color-effect.

But we return to the most remarkable paragraph in Miss Allen's book, in which she says: "If an artist shuts out every thought and idea which do not spring from the physical sense of sight, if he is to make himself into a living eye, impersonal, uncritical, the result will certainly be a very fresh transcription of the world around him. It will be surprisingly lucid and even brutally frank. It will have the additional quality of being expressed in a universal language which all men can read, the language of the physical eye. . . . This is a basis, a standard of comparison which provides the strongest weapon of impressionism. It relies upon the integrity of a single sense. But the very limitations of its unassailable position ensured the strong reaction of expressionism. Physical eyesight is not vision. It deals with an instantaneous impression. Thought is unnecessary, so is experience. Analysis of the immediate optical impressions in terms of paint is all that is required of the impressionist. Needless to say this is no easy task. It requires remarkable powers of differentiation and control, but the result is certainly a simple and limited one. Individual expression is reduced to a minimum. Impressionism is the voice of a universal human sense and nothing more." Generous as is Miss Allen's concession to the difficulties of the task imposed by Impressionism upon the artist, we nevertheless feel that both thought and experience are to be recommended in any undertaking. It were indeed a magnificent technical method by which a work of art might be achieved without either. One might even inquire where the "remarkable powers of differentiation and control" were to come from, if not from these very things?

Undismayed, the weavers of theory continue to weave after the manner of the works we have just reviewed. Of the mystification and confusion they cause the student and the layman they take no account, or are, perhaps, unaware. The conclusions they advance are uncalled for, nor is there any excuse for classifying works according to theories which are in themselves untenable.

The term "Impressionist" is used today by writers to include the works of many painters from the Renaissance to the twentieth century. For example, Thomas Craven says: "The history of Impressionism is the story of the errant struggles of an art that had lost its function, of the path of painting from the church and the public to the dealer and the museum." Mr. Craven continues: "The first artist to deal practically with the analysis of natural light was Titian

when, as he approached the grave and peered at the
world with half-closed eyes, he discovered that light
falling upon objects breaks up the surfaces into patches
of tone . . . Titian's methods were studied in Madrid
by Velasquez, the most marvellous eye in painting.
Velasquez . . . had but one aim: verisimilitude, or
the illusion of the appearance of objects from a single
point of focus and under natural lighting."

But all art is to some degree impressionistic, just as
the same art is to some degree expressionistic. That is
to say, the artist is impressed with certain aspects of
things which have appealed to his mind and which
his imagination has caused him to visualize. These
things he expresses in his chosen medium in his particular way. There is no need to use a term coined to
specify a particular method to cover a general condition. It leads only to one result which we have already
seen—an ingenious elaboration of theory as false as it
is ludicrous; the pursuit of verbal fancy down blind
alleys ending in meaningless confusion. Why it is that
a small group of lesser artists, at the end of the nineteenth century, should assume such an important
place in the minds of theorists is only explicable because theory verbally expressed could, without scruple
in thought, be turned to the advantage of the literary
mind. Of this Mr. Craven's phrases are an example
in point. Apprehended "indistinctly as through a mist"
their meaning assumes an entirely "false magnitude."

It is indeed unintelligible. What are "patches of tone," and what is "the illusion of the appearance of objects from a single point of focus"?

We have seen that in France, at the end of the nineteenth century, a small group of men with similar ambitions were called, by the outside world, Impressionists. With the exception of Renoir, whose scope was wider, Pissarro, Monet, Sisley, whose works are representative, were artists who within a limited horizon pursued a certain course to its conclusion, each in his own way. Because their works were weak in form, and because Cézanne said that he wanted to make something solid and enduring of Impressionism, writers on art appear to take it for granted that by the end of the nineteenth century the whole of the art of painting had become formless. Upon so false a basis theories of mechanistic and scientific method in art might easily flourish; nor would there be difficulty, with such a beginning, in developing further theories of a breakdown of tradition and the search for a new kind of form by twentieth-century non-traditional painters.

It is recorded by Ambroise Vollard, in speaking of the Impressionists, that Renoir said to him: "Why will people continue to see only theorists in these painters whose sole idea, like that of the old masters, has been to paint with fresh and vivid color?"

CHAPTER FOUR

CÉZANNE

PAUL CÉZANNE is one of the pathetic figures of history.

He was a solitary being. What practical experience of painting he acquired as a young man came largely through the Impressionist painters with whom he associated early in his career. His love of nature was as great as theirs, but his point of view differed, as his style differed from their style.

His biographers tell us that he was only occasionally present at the meetings in the Café Guerbois. He was shy and ill at ease with people, and the talk, which was clever and sparkling at these gatherings, exasperated him. He contributed little to the conversation and often sat for hours in a corner by himself, only to leave hastily in an outburst of wrath if something that was said annoyed him. He cherished his independence of mind and lived in great fear of entanglements of any kind. His being was out of harmony with life and maladjusted within itself, so much so that he was all but inarticulate, even in his chosen medium. To Ambroise Vollard he said: "You will understand, Monsieur Vollard, that I have a little sensation, but that I am unable to express it. I am as one who, possessing a gold-piece, is unable to make use of it."

His mind could not assimilate nor his talents transmit to canvas all that his intensely stimulated emotions sought to bring forth. For he did seek, with simple and ardent concentration, to present that which he saw and felt in nature. The manner in which his works are presented bears witness to the inadequacy of his powers of co-ordination; but their substance is often convincing in spite of that manner—and not because of it. His painting is, as he was himself, crude, childlike, and unskilled. It is his unskilled manner which later painters have taken and carried far afield, not the substance of his painting—that they could not take by any means for it is individual and remains elusive, as history shows has ever been the way with works of art.

But Cézanne's gifts were evident despite his strangely inadequate manner of painting—a discrepancy difficult to understand. The world has been at a loss to understand it and has, in consequence, attempted to translate his inadequacy into a new power of expression. And to rationalize that power it has turned to theory and to the painter's own words for further comprehension. In so doing it has misrepresented both and has tried to impose upon Cézanne's works a character he would have disdained; for he said that the importance of a work lies not in its intention, nor in what is said about it, but in its *realization*.

Cézanne's thoughts, expressed in his own words, are those of an artist absorbed in his task and are neither abstract nor mystifying. The following paragraph from a letter to Émile Bernard contains the famous phrase, often quoted but much more often misquoted in contemporary writings, which artists and writers alike have wrapped in mystery. "Let me repeat what I told you here: you must see in nature the cylinder, the sphere, the cone, all put into perspective, so that every side of an object, of a plane, recedes to a central point. The parallel lines at the horizon give the extension, that is, a section of nature, or, if you prefer, of the spectacle which the Pater omnipotens aeterne Deus spreads before our eyes. The perpendicular lines at the horizon give the depth. Now to us nature appears more in depth than in surface, hence the necessity for the introduction into our vibrations of light, represented by reds and yellows, of enough blue tones to make the atmosphere perceptible."

These words, considered in their context as they

should be, suggest a simple and elementary thought, naïvely stated, in which there lies no novelty. It would be difficult to find meaning in them beyond the painter's desire, evident in his best works, to feel the depth and solidity in nature's forms and to seek an expression of their unity, their simplicity, as these qualities are felt when seen in the sphere, the cone, the cylinder, in their undisguised and obvious third dimension. Cézanne's works bespeak the intensity of his feeling for these qualities in nature. They are the source of the vital character of his compositions. But neither the styles of painting of his so-called followers, nor those further developments of style of twentieth-century non-traditional painters, have in any way expressed this understanding. They have all ignored the lesson of his works and have, instead, made travesties of his words. Cézanne was not primarily a theorist. He was a creative artist who felt, observed, thought, and painted first, and spoke his feelings, his observations and his thoughts long afterwards. Therein lies the essential difference between him and his imitators, who are theorists first and last.

The misquoting and misrepresentation in contemporary writing of the things Cézanne has said, more particularly of his phrase about the cylinder, the sphere, the cone, are incredible. Thomas Craven in *Modern Art* has a chapter bearing the title "Cubes and Cones," in which he writes of Cézanne's "painful experiments in cubic structure." Mary Cecil Allen, in *Painters of the Modern Mind*, speaks of his "interpretation of the relations of cubes, cones and cylinders to visible nature." Henry Rankin Poor, in *Modern Art, Why, What and How*, refers to Cézanne's remark that "all forms are reducible to the cube, the cylinder and the cone." James Johnson Sweeney, in *Plastic Redirections in Twentieth Century Painting*, says: "In Cézanne we have a sense of the constituent cones, spheres and cubes beneath the natural form. It was this that made Cézanne so popular when the Cubists were feeling their way back to structure by analytic methods."

What havoc a little imagination may create!

In not one of his several biographies, nor in the many letters written toward the end of his life, nor in any recorded conversations between him and his friends, is the word *cube* mentioned by Cézanne. It has been suggested that this was accidental, perhaps a simple oversight; that having spoken of the cylinder, the sphere, the cone, he could not possibly have meant to omit the cube. Did he then forget it? Or was the omission intentional? Let us consider the phrase once more: "*you must see in nature, the cylinder, the sphere, the cone . . .*" Now, when we look at nature, we see, at every turn, forms which suggest in part the cylinder, the sphere, the cone, quite obviously. But, with the naked eye, cubic forms are not to be seen in nature—although they exist in crystalline form and may be seen through a microscope—and this would seem the best possible reason for Cézanne's lack of mention of the cube as a form to be seen in nature. The massed groups of houses we see in his landscapes, the tables in his still-lifes, are man-made forms, mostly rectangular solids (parallelepipeds), which, although derived from the cube, are seldom cubic. Can we be wrong, then, if we conclude that his failure to mention the cube as one of nature's forms was intentional? In the little lecture on perspective which follows his supposedly cryptic admonition he says that nature appears more to us in depth than in surface. This thought he would naturally apply to any solid form. That he applied it consistently is apparent in his works; but that he was not uniformly successful in its application is also apparent. The terms in which he couched it verbally can only have been intended to emphasize an ancient conception. But to generalize the conception does not excuse misquotation on the part of writers, or the elaborate fabrication of theory upon a false basis. In further explaining his meaning in directing Bernard's attention to the three solids, he said: "One must teach oneself to paint by the study of simple forms—after that one can do whatever one wishes." The purpose for which Cézanne intended his advice would seem quite clear. Nor was the advice in any sense new. Solids have been used in teaching students for many generations. It is interesting to note that in the 1880's, a generation before Cézanne was known to the world, Thomas Eakins, in Philadelphia, made his students draw and paint from eggs for, he said, if a man can draw and paint an egg he can paint anything.

But we must turn our attention once more to cubes, for there is a widespread impression that the so-called "abstract" art of cubism derives from Cézanne's verbally expressed theories of the art of painting, as well as from the example of his works. We are told by Thomas Craven in *Modern Art* that "though playful at times, Cézanne's ventures into cubism were serious enough; and his experiments considered as such, were legitimate and beneficial." Because of Cézanne's words, much has been made of his supposed preoccupation with "abstract form," with "cubism" and "cubic structure," but no one has yet made clear what these may be in relation to the art of painting. "Abstract form" would, indeed, appear to be a contradiction in terms. But "cubism" and "cubic structure"— why not cylinderism, or conism, or spheric structure? The one is no more applicable to Cézanne's works than the other. Let us refer once more to Cézanne's own words: perhaps they can throw light on these mystifications.

Over and over again, and in many different ways, he says that a painter cannot be "too scrupulous, too sincere or too humble before nature," that he must "devote himself entirely to the study of nature and try to produce pictures that have real meaning." Not only does he harp upon this subject in his letters to the two young painters Émile Bernard and Charles Camoin, but he gives definite warning against an artist becoming involved in abstractions. He says, for instance: "The artist should scorn any opinion that is not based on an intelligent observation of character. He should avoid the literary spirit, which so often leads the painter astray from his real mission, the concrete study of nature—and causes him to lose himself for too long at a time among intangible speculations." And again: "To talk about art is almost useless. The labor which brings about progress in one's own calling is sufficient compensation for a lack of comprehension on the part of fools. The 'littérateur' expresses himself by means of abstractions, the true painter by means of design and color, his sensations and perceptions." Also, he says: "One is able to talk more, and perhaps better, about painting when one is in front of one's motif, than when one hazards purely speculative theories— in which one very often goes astray." He said he did not desire to be in the right theoretically, but in the presence of nature. And again: "There must be imitation, and a little illusion of actuality (*trompe l'oeil*) can do no harm, if there is art in the way it is done." He also warns the painter not to try to make other people's theories his own, for then he becomes only an imitator.

Desperately in earnest, Cézanne labored constantly and tirelessly in his study of nature. What, then, was his preoccupation with cubic structure? This question remains unanswered after reading many books upon the subject. Such preoccupation is not to be seen in his works; it is not to be noted in his words. It would, indeed, appear that his mind was profoundly occupied with a painter's problems and that such a childish notion as this had escaped him.

What we do see in his works was an heroic attempt to present what was, to him, the essential character of nature's forms. But he was insufficiently equipped for his chosen task. His works are broken fragments of what he hoped to achieve; fragments with qualities of greatness, not realizations of his desire. We know that few artists feel that their works fully realize their intentions (even the conceited also have their doubts). Apart from Cézanne's own words, his inability to realize as he would have liked is evident in his works.

That he deliberately distorted his forms to reach a truer expression of his intention is scarcely credible. It is, indeed, such a notion as he would have warned against as belonging to the literary spirit. His mind was a constructive mind, and distortion can serve no constructive purpose. Distortion of form is a breaking down of form. Émile Bernard states that he had thought the defects of Cézanne's works were due to voluntary negligence, but found that Cézanne himself attributed them to faulty eyesight: forms were often blurred, he said, and straight lines fell away.

The recorded conversations by Émile Bernard together with Cézanne's letters to him and to Charles Camoin, appear to form the chief verbal sources from which the world today draws inspiration for theorizing about Cézanne's works. It is scarcely possible not to note that Cézanne's own words are those of a man absorbed in the endeavor to paint what he sees. Émile Bernard's words, on the contrary, make a different impression. He frequently appears to urge Cézanne into some verbally expressed theory which may, perchance, solve the riddle presented by his works. For example, in the *Mercure de France* (June 1, 1921), "A Conversation With Cézanne," Émile Bernard reports that he said to Cézanne during the course of one of their walks in the environs of Aix:

"You, then, conceive art as a union of the Universe and the individual?"

"I conceive it as a personal apperception. I place this apperception in sensation and I demand of the intelligence to organize it with purpose (l'organizer en oeuvre)."

"But of which sensations do you speak? Of those of your feeling (sentiment) or of those of your retina?"

"I think there should be no distinction between these; as I am a painter I hold to the visual sensation above all."

"You are, then, like Zola, of the naturalist school."

"I want to be a painter, and I depend upon my eye to make a picture which appeals to the eye."

Cézanne's verbally expressed ideal was to give to the world, in his own way, his realization of his "little sensation," and through it the love he felt for nature and the achievements of the great masters in painting—"to realize as did the Venetians." Could his own words be brought to the attention of the student, and the haze of mystification with which writers on aesthetics have surrounded them be dispelled, the thoughts of a wise and simple counselor would be at his disposal. He believed that an artist should be a workman in his art and know early in his career his method of realization—that he should be a painter "by the intrinsic qualities of painting and make good use of its rich materials." It is not difficult to imagine the disgust Cézanne would have felt had he known that his works were to be considered experiments in "cubic structure"—compositions conceived as abstractions.

He had a tragically keen sense of his own ineffectualness and was beset by the fear that his "little sensation" would be taken from him by outsiders, ever ready, as he thought, to break the delicate thread of his mind's contact with it. He spoke decisively of his imitators. In 1904, two years before his death, M. Bernard said to him: "Gauguin likes your painting very much and has imitated you." To which Cézanne replied: "That is all very well, but he has not understood me. I have never tolerated and I shall never accept his lack of modelling or gradation (graduation). It is nonsense. Gauguin is not a painter—'Il ne fait que des images chinoises!'" And when Bernard spoke to him of those pretended "continuateurs" at Paris who were succeeding so well, with so few qualities, in fooling the public, particularly the Germans, Cézanne replied: "All that is of no account; those people are farceurs."

We said in an earlier chapter that the artist, preoccupied with his own idea, is not a revolutionary spirit—he does not advance in the art of painting by revolting against what does not interest him, against what will not suit his purpose. He is interested in making, not in destroying. Theodore Duret, a contemporary of the Impressionists and of Cézanne, says of the latter: "Of all the remarkable facts in connection with Cézanne's life and work, the most remarkable was the astonishing contrast which existed between the popular estimation of the man and his true character. The man whose art was denounced as that of a communard and an anarchist was in reality a rich bourgeois, conservative, Catholic, who never suspected that anyone would ever take him for a revolutionary, who devoted all his time to his work, who led the most regular life and was worthy of all esteem."

Cézanne's conservatism expressed itself in another way. It was his great desire to be received at the "Salon de Bouguereau," but he said he knew very well what was the obstacle to that end. "It is because I do not sufficiently realize; we have not eyes for nothing." It was his wish to see a canvas of his own hung in the Louvre beside those works of art which formed his highest ideal. And to crown his life and to reward his labors he longed to be decorated by the Institut des Beaux Arts. But these things were not to be.

In 1902 M. Roujon, then director of the Beaux Arts, when approached by M. Mirbeau on the subject of a decoration for Cézanne, said: "Alas, my dear Mirbeau, in as much as I am director of the Beaux

Arts, I must follow the public taste and not precede it." And then: "Monet, if you wish. Monet does not want it? Then take Sisley. What, is he dead? Do you wish Pissarro?" And, misconstruing Mirbeau's silence, "Is he dead too? Then choose whomever you will, but promise you will speak to me no more of this Cézanne."

At the age of sixty-seven, one month before his death, Cézanne wrote: "Shall I ever reach the goal so eagerly sought and so long pursued? I hope so, but so long as it has not been attained a vague feeling of discomfort persists which will not disappear until I shall have gained the harbour, that is, until I shall have accomplished something more promising than what has gone before, thereby verifying my theories which, in themselves, are easy to put forth. The only thing which is really difficult is to prove what one believes. So I am going on with my researches.

"But I have just reread your letter and I see that I am answering it very indirectly. You will kindly forgive me; as I have told you, the reason is my preoccupation with the goal to be attained. I am continually making observations from nature and I feel that I am making some slight progress. I should like to have you here with me, for my solitude always oppresses me a little; but I am old, ill, and I have sworn to die painting rather than sink into the nasty corruption that threatens old men who allow themselves to be dominated by degrading passions. If I ever have the pleasure of being with you again some day, we can discuss things more easily by word of mouth.

"You will forgive me for harping constantly on the same string, but I am progressing toward the logical development of *what we see and feel by studying nature; a consideration of processes comes later, processes being for us nothing but simple methods for making the public feel what we ourselves feel, and for making ourselves intelligible. The masters we admire can have done no more than that.*" (Author's italics.)

That quality which distinguishes the works of great men—one which words cannot touch—Cézanne had in common with the great masters in the art of painting. But their powers of realization were denied him and he knew it, for he said: "I shall remain the primitive of the way I have discovered."

Did Cézanne discover a way?

If he did, it has been ignored by his followers. He desired no more than to make his "sensations and perceptions" intelligible to others in the painter's medium, but this much he did desire. That his way of doing this was not clear, even to himself, is evident in his works. Because it was not clear, the outside world sought further indication of its direction in his words. But these have been so overlaid with meaningless phraseology by writers in pursuit of false-scented trails that the true qualities in his works, there for the eye to see, are scarcely noted. To heed the distorted outpourings of the literary spirit which tells us that twentieth-century non-traditional cults in painting find their source in the example of Cézanne, is to do Cézanne dishonor.

Empty phrases founded on misconceptions lead nowhere. To imitate the manner of another is not to follow in his footsteps. But, if we try to understand the single-minded, earnest artist, whose sole desire was to render what he saw and felt in nature, if we are willing to see where he failed, and why, we may find the way toward which he pointed.

CHAPTER FIVE

SUGGESTION OR FULFILLMENT

IT has been said in these pages that tradition embodies the learning and the wisdom of the past and indicates the course of future thought; that it is a learning of infinitely wider scope than the mere knowledge of forms, methods, modes of painting, necessarily limited, taught in the schools of any period; it is a learning fundamentally connected with the strange human necessity to create, with the innate love of beauty and the harassing desire for perfection. These are facts difficult to admit in a day when ideas of order and beauty are lightly cast aside as outmoded; a day in which science is probing, analyzing, cataloguing the mysteries of the nature of man, calling his instincts by confusing if enlightened names. Nevertheless these facts should be admitted lest we forget entirely how it is an artist becomes an artist. For it would seem, today, that the more we learn of the human being the more we permit our knowledge to obscure our understanding of his art. We are all too prone to forget, as is science herself, that she cannot define for the artist's use that which is indefinable.

It is well to note that throughout man's recorded history outstanding achievement in the arts has resulted from a profound and unself-conscious absorption of the artist in his subject—an attitude which brought forth from great men works of highly individual character. The artist's instinct is to make, and his desire is to bring the making to conclusion in an entity. His works are the result of his interest in his idea. His intention is to create an image as like to the image he has conceived as mortal may attain. Therefore conviction enters his works, and the greater his power of mind over his materials the greater and the more convincing will be the realization of his intention. His works are not the result of theory as to the nature of his idea nor of his style of execution. Theory may suggest his procedure but it does not direct its purpose; it remains subservient to it. His presentation is of such an order that all who behold may see what he has seen—may understand how he has seen it. It is he who renews the knowledge and the wisdom of the world; who keeps it perpetually vital.

To this class of artist the Impressionists proper and Cézanne belong; for their works are, in their different ways, vital contributions to the art of painting. Besides the works themselves, the Impressionists' theories of color had a widespread influence on painters everywhere.

Cézanne's contribution is far more difficult to estimate than that of the Impressionists, because the true lesson of his works has been obscured by constant discussion of his theories. It is believed, for instance, that because he perceived so largely through the channels of his emotions, his works show a greater sensitiveness to and a keener statement of essentials than the works of his contemporaries and even of his predecessors. Theorists have gone so far as to state that Cézanne re-established, in an art lost in a haze of superficialities, the significance of the third dimension. But the art of painting was not lost in any such haze. Manet, Degas, Forain, who were Cézanne's contemporaries, Ingres, who came just before him, were all greater masters of form than he; all possessed as keen a sense of the significance of the third dimension. These things become evident in a comparison of the widely differing works of these five artists.

That Cézanne failed to "realize" by means of representational form can scarcely be less than obvious, not because he scorned its limitations or considered them inadequate to his purpose, as his biographers would have one believe, but because of his lack of co-ordination between intellect and emotion, the great stumbling block which thwarted his genius throughout his life. Cézanne's great desire was, on the contrary, to "realize" as did the old masters; but he himself, as we have seen, recognized his failure and the reasons for it. Let us recall his many portraits and figure compositions: the portrait of Ambroise Vollard, for instance, famous for its one hundred and fifteen sittings, as childish and inept a work as could come from a painter's brush. Or the large canvases of bathers, naïvely suggested compositions, inadequate from any point of view. Even in the pictures of the card players, which are superb examples of his ability to compose and the best of his figure paintings, he has not mastered representational form.

But his failure was not the usual one, that is, subsidence into the commonplace—what writers today call photographic art. His preoccupation with his conceptions, grand in their simplicity, prevented such failure. The inevitable result of his artless execution was that he was forced to work by means of space arrangement. He could not work in any other way. That is to say: he could not mold form, therefore choice of pattern became the only means of rendering his ideas— emphasis upon the pattern, not upon the forms of which the pattern is composed. Or, let us say it thus: his form was achieved through his selective powers of composition, not by mastery of the forms which made the composition. His wholehearted concentration

upon what were to him the important aspects of nature, his extraordinary capacity for keeping essentials
always before him, his selection of and emphasis upon
these, gave his design its vital character.

Now, the ability to use space arrangement, that is,
to carry it beyond mere composition to a fuller realization of his desires, is a test of an artist's powers. In
this manner he succeeds, or fails, to convey emotional
intensity. Color, which to most people is the first
medium of emotional expression, is subject to the
same principles of presentation. Without a chosen
emphasis no work conveys its meaning. Through his
emphasis upon composition Cézanne's emotions
found expression in pictorial form.

Not content to accept these things at their face
value, though they are the self-evident characteristics
of Cézanne's works, theorists have seized upon his
artlessness and called it a deliberate attempt to express
himself by means of "abstract" form. But Cézanne
was too unsophisticated, too deeply in earnest, his desires too profoundly simple and too sincere for this
kind of artifice. Moreover, for a true painter, there
can be no satisfaction in the limitations such artifice
imposes.

But their constructive contributions to the art of
painting are, alas, not all that the Impressionists and

Cézanne left to posterity, for in some ways they contributed to its follies also.

Their theories have been elaborated in the twentieth century far beyond these painters' own conceptions of their use, and have served more to misrepresent artistic achievement than to clarify its mysteries. Their obtrusive styles of painting have created a precedent for incomplete presentation. Even though Cézanne's style is fragmentary, and Monet's obvious, both men at their best presented part of a consistent whole, and, because what they "saw" was "seen," that is, conceived, in its entirety, that part presents an appearance of truth. Because of this their works are of importance, not because of their theories or their methods. But, because of their theories, their incomplete modes of presentation were adopted far and wide by painters, and by the devoted amateur who felt that through their example the art of painting had come within his grasp.

Works of distinction are always imitated. Let us see what occurred after Cézanne and after Monet, a man of less great potentialities but of more consistent achievement.

Monet's following of imitators was a large one, but the number of imitators Cézanne had in the first quarter of this century is unprecedented for any painter. It became popular after the Impressionists to paint overcolored pictures in an undiscriminating, spotty technique; but Cézanne's works encouraged a flood of inept productions lacking in both color-discrimination and form. Before his death the "farceurs" in Paris had drawn attention to themselves, and a little later cubism, and the many "ists" and "isms" which accompanied and followed it, overran the world. The Impressionist way of painting remained distinct, while the rest became a meaningless confusion.

The inherent weakness of Monet's and Cézanne's works is to be found in their obtrusive styles. Each painter's technique is a predominant characteristic of his product. Each painter undertook to reach as difficult a goal, against as great odds, as a painter can set himself; but neither conquered the means by which he sought to reach it—the raw materials of his art. With Monet, preoccupied with effects of color, the handling of pigments in a technique too obvious made color too apparent as variety of colors. Cézanne, groping for realization in an inadequate technique, obvious because maladroit, caused doubt and speculation as to his intentions.

Because the Impressionist manner of painting is a severely limited means of expression, those who adopted it achieved nothing further with it than had been achieved by the Impressionists themselves. It lends itself only to theoretical exaggeration.

Cézanne's manner of painting is, possibly, an even more limited means of expression than the Impressionists'. But Cézanne, because of his single-minded intensity of purpose, made his conception visually felt and recognizable in spite of it. This his imitators, who borrowed his technique but lacked his purpose, have consistently failed to do. Their works are theorized contrivances, not visualized conceptions. Therefore verbal explanation of their intentions became necessary in an attempt to bestow what their works lacked of visual form.

In the works of the masters of the past we see painting and sculpture which not only conveys an impression of truth through its form but which also creates a standard of accomplishment. These two characteristics appear in visual presentation. We see them clearly in the painting and sculpture of prehistoric and primitive peoples, in the arts of Egypt and Greece, of China and Japan and of the Western world. In all of them the artist has worked toward perfection, to render his idea with the greatest skill possible in the use of his materials that its form might reach fulfillment in a beauty realized.

The non-traditional painter of today, and his advocates, explain the absence of such form in his works by the assertion that the lack of it only indicates a deeper search for the essential character of form; that the abandonment of traditional form liberates the artist from its fetters and frees him to create a more profound, a more expressive art. But to abandon traditional form and to substitute for it form which is not intelligible—form which is not form but only shape— to embrace the void, as it were, is not only not instinctive nor in any sense freeing to the spirit; it is, on the contrary, arbitrary and limits the artist's powers and is in the poorest sense artificial. It is not art, but artifice.

Incompleteness of presentation is not undesirable in itself, but its success depends upon the kind of incompleteness. The briefest sketch may be a summary of the artist's thought and feeling—that is, it may state the essentials of his idea. When it does so it is as desirable a performance in its way as the far-carried picture.

The twentieth-century non-traditional painter says there is a greater suggestiveness in incomplete presentation than in attempted realization; that to try to bring a work to conclusion is more than likely to destroy its imaginative qualities. It was different with the old traditional painter, as indeed it is different with the modern traditional painter. These could, and can, present, in their completed works, without fear of loss in the attempt, the same essentials as their sketches displayed—and by completed is meant as full a realization of the artist's conception as he felt he had been able to give. These artists could preserve their thought and build upon its vitality until they wrought a work more poignant and expressive than the sketch. This the non-traditional painter has failed to do; failed because his brief manner is merely brief and not suggestive, his crudenesses merely crude and not a sign either of strength of purpose or of emotional intensity. And this is because his mind is directed toward verbal theorizing—he is not a painter first, but a theorist first. When he shows us his quasi-geometrical forms he *tells* us that these express the "cubic content," the "fundamental structure of the object," with greater meaning and insight into the character of nature's forms than the mere imitation (or what he calls "reproduction") of "surface appearances" could do. When the trunk of a tree is presented in cylindrical form with lesser cylinders for branches he *tells* us that what we see is the essential form of a tree—a rendering of its spirit rather than its substance. Because words are the non-traditional artist's first preoccupation he forgets that surface appearance is a manifestation of original form; that the two are one and the same and that it is his business to find a way to make this visually apparent so that without words we may sense the spirit of his work. But, after a quarter century of verbal explanation of his intention, his works are still being verbally explained. His forms, evolved from formulae, have become stereotyped through constant repetition. They are always the same commonplace, uninspired shapes—presentations of the limited conceptions of the mediocre mind, not of the essential character of form. It is little wonder that such minds cannot pursue their works beyond the first statement, for in their theory there is no vitality upon which to build. Nor is it any wonder the non-traditional artist believes an attempt to carry his first statement further would be to destroy its finest qualities.

It cannot be too often repeated that painting and sculpture are visual arts. As we use words with commonly accepted meanings to make our thoughts and emotions understood by our fellows, so the shapes of things ordinarily encountered in our daily life must be the means by which an artist makes known his thoughts and feelings.

The recognizable form in which painting and sculpture have always been executed is called representational—a term today used in a derogatory sense, as though the sights familiar in daily life, and therefore recognizable, were on that account necessarily commonplace and inferior as a means of expression. The words the poet uses to make poetry are for the most part those the ordinary man uses in his undistinguished daily intercourse, but they are not therefore an inferior means to the poet's end; nor because they are so familiar and have been so much used, is their use as a medium outworn; nor, again because poets have reached great heights of expression in their medium, has all been achieved that ever can be achieved therein.

Similarly, in painting and sculpture, it is not the use of representational form which was outworn by the end of the nineteenth century as the artist's means of expression. Rather, the rising generation of artists had slighter gifts and minds not sufficiently creative to raise their performance much above the commonplace. To remedy a situation keenly felt by many among them the more ingenious turned to the invention of theories to supply the vitality lacking in their gifts. In such conditions theories grow rank as weeds and before long obscure all evidence of creative thought. Because the forms chosen for their development were arbitrary and unnatural, they were visually inadequate and needed verbal explanation.

Thus, after the turn of the twentieth century, the great majority of artists, led by an adroit few (outstanding among them Matisse and Picasso), who sought escape from mediocrity in a reign of fads, were guided by theory. The precedent for disorder and ugliness established by them is merely a cloak for the weak and ineffectual and is not a manifestation of strength or a new form of art. The disguise has persisted over a long period of time because it is inspired by a kind of thought which holds the imagination in its grip at the same time that it falsifies artistic issues in a phraseology which is suggestive, if irrelevant and obscure in meaning. The form in which these works are presented is, in fact, decadent, but it is called abstract and because it is not recognizable it is accompanied by an explanatory language in praise of qualities not visually perceptible. Abstract qualities have, in themselves, no recognizable form and therefore they must, if they are to be understood, be embodied in some known form which is recognizable. The large majority of works exhibited today are executed in ignorance of the uses to which the artist's materials may and should be put. Only by the few who are innovators, and whose intention seems to be conscious obscuration, have they been ingeniously devised in pretense of meaning.

Theorists today, painters and writers alike, have lost their sense of direction. They appear to be entangled more deeply than ever before in a maze of words and phrases, battling with the chimera of abstract form on the one hand, and the terrifying, inescapable reality of representational form on the other. Through the haze of mystification and confusion which they create our attention is arrested by what appears, in most painters today, to be a different attitude of mind from that of Cézanne and his contemporaries; an attitude which also contrasts sharply with that of artists of preceding centuries; an attitude the reverse of creative, for it is essentially analytical. Not analytical in the objective sense when artists analyzed the practical problems connected with their art, but analytical in a different way. Most painters today are intent upon *self-expression* and try to think in terms of *self-analysis*. But, even though the artist's work is inevitably the result of self-expression, self-expression is not the artist's conscious concern. When he attempts conscious self-expression he also attempts self-analysis and thus, when with mind turned inward he attempts to paint, he invariably meets with disaster. To save himself and to explain what it was he desired to express, he resorts to words. And to help him to his goal, philosophers, psychologists, psychoanalysts, have all contributed their findings. But their knowledge has not proved of the kind to produce a more expressive art than has hitherto been known. It has not aided in the production of works convincing in themselves, works which require no verbal explanation of the artist's intention. This is not surprising: it is, on the contrary, inevitable, for analysis of abstract qualities brings about their negation.

In order to bring a work of art into being it is necessary that the tangible and the intangible should function in harmony; that there may be a balance between what the artist seeks to know about his subject and that which must remain unknown to him, unquestioned by him, of himself, in order that those creative powers which "may be witnessed but not weighed" may truly function. This does not mean that the artist creates only when moved by impulse, as so many people think, or by inspiration, as it is called—and that this impulse must not be interfered with by the thinking mind. The contrary is the case. His attention should be directed upon his subject by every power he possesses, but it should not be directed upon himself, in self-examination; he should not, as it were, watch himself in a mirror, with the expectation of discovering those qualities of which his impulse, his inspiration, his creative instinct, is composed. He would then lose himself for too long in that intangible speculation which Cézanne predicted would lead him astray. Nevertheless, this is the vain pursuit of the many in art today—an attempt to define qualities in themselves indefinable—a contradiction sufficient to nullify their efforts, for expression so attempted is invariably assumed, and therefore false. Instead of resulting in works of highly individual character, these efforts result only in works without originality or meaning; the gropings of bewildered, misdirected minds. The endeavor to present abstract qualities in concrete form ends always in the same way: in works which have to be explained in words, which are themselves, as painting and sculpture, nothing.

We have seen a little of the traditional artist's attitude toward his work and also a little of the non-traditional artist's attitude toward his. We have also seen something of what the writer on art makes of the traditional artist's works by means of theory, and presently we shall see what he makes of the non-traditional artist's works, by the same means.

Before we do this, however, let us turn to Alfred H. Barr of New York's Modern Museum, who in his book *Cubism and Abstract Art* has made a most courageous attempt to explain the meaning of *abstract* in relation to works of art. It runs as follows: "The verb to abstract means to draw out of or away from. But the noun abstraction is already drawn out of or away from—so much so that like a geometrical figure or an amorphous silhouette it may have no apparent relation to concrete reality. 'Abstract' is therefore an adjective which may be applied to works within a certain latitude. . . ." Again, "abstract art today needs no defense. It has become one of the many ways to paint or carve or model. It is based upon the assumption that a work of art, a painting for example, is worth looking at primarily because it presents a composition, or organization of color, line, light and shade. Resemblance to natural objects, while it does not necessarily destroy these aesthetic values, may easily adulterate their purity. Therefore, since resemblance to nature is at best superfluous, and at worst distracting, it might as well be eliminated. . . ." "Pure abstractions are those in which the artist makes a composition of abstract elements, such as geometrical or amorphous shapes. Near-abstractions are compositions in which the artist, starting with natural forms, transforms them into abstract or nearly abstract forms. He approaches an abstract goal but does not quite reach it. . . ." "The ambiguity of the word abstract as applied to works of art is really useful, for it reveals the ambiguity and confusion which is inseparable from the subject."

But do we *really* need to know that the ambiguity of the word abstract is really useful? Do we need one ambiguity to reveal another, only in the end to confirm the confusion from which we hoped to emerge? Mr. Barr has been consoled by the dictionary, but its consolations have not survived the length of his effort at elucidation. Works of art, paintings for example, have always been worth looking at primarily because they were compositions—or organizations, if we prefer contemporary English usage—of line, color, light and shade, presenting an artist's thought and feeling, and have enjoyed world-wide acceptance as works of art upon that basis without ambiguity or confusion. But, if ambiguity and confusion are qualities inseparable from abstract works, how in the name of art did these works come to be called compositions or organizations? That which is ambiguous or confused is not composed or organized.

Shall we, in our art of the future, have form, confused, ambiguous, whose meaning has to be suggested in words because it is not to be seen by the eye; a painting and sculpture in which form and idea are severed because the artist is thinking in words and not in his own medium? Or shall we have works which are "the logical development of what we see and feel by the study of nature" as Cézanne desired; works in which the artist's idea may be seen in concrete form?

CHAPTER SIX

ABSTRACT ART

IN pointing to the fallacies of our contemporary theorists on matters concerning the arts of painting and sculpture, it is well to observe once more that we are not dealing with a novel subject. Such fallacies have come into being gradually because the human mind is ever fascinated by verbal speculation and because it is unwilling to let speculative thought rest as such within its own sphere, but must attempt to make it a guide to artistic appreciation if not to a practice of the arts.

To Plato's Socrates philosophy spelled the highest form of learning, or knowledge. He said: "And when persons who are unworthy of education approach philosophy and make an alliance with her who is in a rank above them, what sort of ideas and opinions are likely to be generated? Will they not deserve to be called sophisms captivating to the ear, having nothing in them genuine, or worthy of, or akin to true wisdom?" This was said in a day when education was not general, when its advantages had not been tendered to the many as it is in this twentieth century.

Since the Middle Ages, philosophers have labored mightily at the erection of immense structures of hypothesis and speculation, building thereby a veritable Tower of Babel—"because the Lord did there confound the language of all the earth." We noted that Sir Joshua Reynolds, one hundred and fifty years ago, deplored the love of mystifying speech about art in his day. Goethe also disapproved of the same sort of thing when, in 1797, he wrote to Schiller: "Such driveling on the principles of art as is now the fashion has doubtless never been known in the history of the world." And today Bertrand Russell calls philosophy "an unusually ingenious attempt to think fallaciously." He says: "The typical philosopher finds certain beliefs emotionally indispensable, but intellectually difficult; he therefore goes through long chains of reasoning, in the course of which, sooner or later, a momentary lack of vigilance allows a fallacy to pass undetected. After the one false step, his mental agility takes him far into the quagmires of falsehood." Unfortunately writers on art, their minds steeped in the specious phraseology of modern philosophic doctrine, all too frequently give evidence of this process also. For example: Sheldon· Cheney, in *Expressionism in Art*, says: "The new philosophies start with two essentially modern conceptions; that life is not static, perfectable and statable, but an evolutionary growth, change, a progress; and that relatedness rather than isolated individuality is basic . . . Modern Painting, on the formal or instrumental side, likewise arrives nearer to understanding of basic principles by study of dynamic relativity. The unity of the creative picture grows out of a poised inter-relation of potentially energetic volumes, each with weight and direction exerting stresses on all the others—they in turn exerting a combined pull on it. The paths of tension are from axis to axis (the axial center being determined by the crossing of the two rotational axes of the volume)." Thus does Mr. Cheney mire himself in the slough of absurdity. Has not the very existence of a work of art always depended upon the "relatedness" of its parts without need of potentially energetic volumes or rotational axes?

Nothing daunted, however, let us examine Mr. Cheney's definition of Expressionism. "Just what, it is fair to ask, does the Modern Artist express? What is revealed in his art, that existed not at all in the average art of the Realistic-Romantic era, or only in very subordinate measure? . . . Expressionism is presentative where Realism is representative; creative where Realism is imitative. From the 19th century view-point Expressionist art is often 'distorted' because camera truth is violated. But the artist claims that he has neglected or distorted lesser truths only to reveal a greater; for the sake of expressing the formal values and intensified feeling of an individualized image."

Mr. Cheney has led us straight into the turmoil with which those who eschew the problems of representational form surround themselves. To impress upon our minds a more fervent picture of Expressionist ideals he quotes from a Dr. Pfister who, he says, has written about the "psychological and biological basis of Expressionism" as follows: "The Expressionist wants to reproduce the intrinsic meaning of things, their soul-substance, but this grasping of the intrinsic, i.e., the only genuine reality, is not done through the intellectual study of the external world. From this view-point impressionism appears as mere surface art, and therefore a superficial art, a mechanical craft and no art at all. The Expressionist on the other hand creates out of the depth of things, because he knows himself to be in those depths. To paint out of himself and to paint himself means to reproduce the intrinsic nature of things, the Absolute. The Artist creates as God creates out of his own inner self and in his own likeness."

And how does the Expressionist do this? Mr. Cheney says "the artist claims he neglects or distorts lesser truths only to reveal a greater." Is it "intrinsic meanings" then—images reproduced in his own like-ness—which we see in the distortions of the Expressionist?

Such theories as this are typical of the sort of argument so many so-called modern artists and writers on art advance in their evasion of the baffling problems which the use of representational form involves. That distortion in art is a breaking down of form by misplaced emphasis which distracts attention wherever it is found, is an obvious condition to which they appear indifferent. Distortion destroys the character and the meaning of form and leaves the beholder bewildered and with a sense of ineffectualness in the artist himself; as though he had suffered frustration of his intention. Speculation always follows as to what his intention may have been, and to avoid misconception he himself, or his spokesman in writing, or both, converse impressively about intrinsic meanings. Meanwhile the distorted shapes in his pictures remain the same distorted shapes, pictorially incomprehensible.

In the art of painting, as in any art, the artist emphasizes what is to him the greater truth and, if he is truly an artist, the lesser truths which he minimizes, or even, perhaps, "neglects," will have served his purpose in that they become unapparent. To distort lesser truths is not to reveal a greater truth but to draw attention to something comparatively unimportant which, because it is distorted, becomes inexplicable and thereby destroys the unity of a work. To "distort lesser truths only to reveal a greater" is as foolish a fancy as words could express.

As an example of its folly, we find in Mary Cecil Allen's book that "The immense feet in a Picasso drawing establish a strong sense of weight and contact with the floor." While we recognize the desirability of establishing weight and contact with the floor for the sake of gravity, such a method only defeats its own end by causing us to laugh. Nor can we guess what greater truth has been revealed in so inept a manner. In the past artists have been highly successful in establishing weight and contact with the floor without giving prominence to a detail *intrinsically* so uninteresting. Miss Allen goes on to say that "Modern Expressionism retains distortion as its special privilege and unconscious virtue." But the contradictory phrases we find in these authors' works cause us to doubt if they have given real thought to their subject.

It is notable that although the abstract artist repudiates the standard which tradition upholds in the matter of representational form, he spends much thought on seeking precedent in the history of art for his theories of distortion, that they may appear to be founded in tradition. He cites Leonardo's drawings of human malformations. But these drawings are not in any sense illustrative of distortion in artistic expression. They are intense, merciless studies of physical distortion, possibly caricatured, but not necessarily so.

El Greco's works are pointed to as another example of historical precedent. And here, indeed, is distortion, but of a character consistent in this painter's works, and notably to their detriment. It is their weakness not their strength. Whether it was deliberate, whether, as is believed today, El Greco employed distortion to intensify emotional effect, nobody knows. The point remains, that had it served his purpose it would not be present in his works *as distortion;* so much energy on the part of theorists would not have been spent attempting to explain it, and at least two-thirds of the books on art of the twentieth century would not have been written. May we not allow a little common sense to enter our speculations and put aside our fear of those who scoff? It has been said that El Greco suffered from defective eyesight. Before the twentieth century it was believed that he did. Is not this possibility perhaps more worthy of consideration than the theories offered in its stead today? Distortion of so consistent a character, although it varies greatly in degree throughout his works, must have some such foundation. El Greco was too brilliant a painter, an artist designed on too grand a scale to employ the same artifice in all his works regardless of monotony and, at times, of absurdity.

And the Surrealist of the 1930's chooses the ingenious works of Hieronymus Bosch and Pieter Breughel with which to compare his efforts in psychological vagary, that these may appear to spring from ancient lineage and thus help him to establish his claim to serious consideration as an artist.

But there is no curbing the speculations of theorists. Even our institutions of learning sponsor their writings. A little publication of the Renaissance Society of the University of Chicago, entitled *The Meaning of Unintelligibility in Modern Art*, by Edward F. Rothschild, contains this paragraph: "Every picture that the Expressionist paints is a self portrait. The object is distorted, disintegrated, or disrupted, by the participating self-projecting, dynamic transcendent subject. This is what is meant by ego-centrism. This is why the Expressionist idiom is explosive, fantastic, violent, centrifugal, or centripetal; its colors bizarre or eerie; its composition dynamic; its texture rough and varied; its rhythms eccentric; its imagery confused or dissociative; its mood electric, thunderous, prestidigitative, or nervous. . . . Expressionism is also characterized by formlessness, but it is motivated by participation, destruction, and dynamism."

Words fail us, as they do not Mr. Rothschild. We

have only the most profound sympathy for the Expressionist in his extreme discomfort.

But what of the more practical side of abstract artistic expression, the artist's way of going about his work? In the preface to *Painters of the Modern Mind*, Mary Cecil Allen causes a painter to interrogate himself, and thus we are enabled to see how the contemporary non-traditional artist conceives the presentation of his thoughts.

"Why do you paint?

Because things I see excite me and I want to reproduce this feeling.

Then if you reproduce visible nature on canvas, you will also reproduce your excitement.

No, because it is not an image but an idea that excites me. It is this idea which I want to realize on my canvas. If I realize the image hoping that it will also realize my idea, it is a travesty because it is only raw material at the end and not an idea at all.

What is your idea then?

It is a conception of natural objects as the directions of planes in space, expressed by lines, colors, lights and shadows, and the arrangements and combinations of these planes in such a way as to produce great pleasure.

Then your picture might not resemble the scene before you at all?

I consider the picture would be based upon the scene in somewhat the same way that variations are based upon a given theme in music. I regard the scene before me as a motive. It determines my choice of lines, colors, lights and shadows.

What is the difference between a good painting and a bad one then? It seems as if the criterion or standard had been removed if we no longer have the power of comparing a painting with nature.

But the painting is not to be compared with visible objects as seen mechanically by the eye. It is to be compared with ideas. The test is whether it realizes them visually or not. The difference between visual realization and the lack of it is the difference between a good and a bad picture."

Miss Allen again disarms us by saying very truly that the difference between a good picture and a bad picture is the difference between visual realization of the artist's idea and the lack of it. But her artist's intentions are stated as the non-traditional artist of today states his—in what Cézanne called the "abstractions" of the "littérateur," not in visual realizations. The result is that they are confused and even contradictory.

Miss Allen's artist says that *things he sees* excite him, and then, that it is not "the *image* but the idea" which excites him. There would seem to be contradiction at this point. To make a statement with one breath and to nullify its value in the next gives instability to the argument. If the artist is excited by things he *sees* then he should not confuse his hearers by contradicting himself and denying the sensations he receives from the image. If he is to realize his idea in the artist's medium he must return to the observer's sense of sight as best he can, in visually realized form, the sensations he receives from the image. If the image does not thus present the artist's idea, nothing else will. In the art of painting the two are inseparable. If the artist denies the image he also denies the idea. Miss Allen has again fallen into confusion by elaborating the popular and pleasing fallacy that there are two ways of "seeing" in the art of painting—one with the mind and the other "mechanically by the eye."

To conceive of natural objects as the directions of planes in space as expressed by lines, colors, lights and shadows is merely to assemble the artist's raw materials—not to present a conception of anything. All works of art are composed of these details, but, as long as they remain visible as *lines, colors, lights and shadows*, any visual realization of the artist's idea, however exciting, is frustrated. Indeed, so immature and so elementary a conception as this to which Miss Allen's artist aspires leaves him seriously under suspicion of having no ideas to present in artistic form.

Let us say this in another way. Let us suppose that our attention has been arrested by the sight of a fine gown. It is the gown which produces our enthusiasm and not the many differently shaped pieces of material, the seams and stitching, with which it is put together. Should these be apparent to the exclusion of its effect upon our sight as a fine gown, we should consider the maker a failure both as a tailor and an artist. We should not hesitate to say he had not realized his idea. Nor would we be at all impressed if he explained the theory upon which he had designed the gown as a conception of objects as shapes in space expressed by seams, stitchings, gores and pleats; our common sense, if not our sense of humor, would prevent our being fooled. But in painting we are blinded by plausible phrases and permit any verbal folly to override our instincts and our judgment.

To consider that the picture would be based upon the scene in *somewhat* the same way that variations are based upon a given theme in music, is to evade the issue. It is as necessary to the realization of a picture that its theme be clearly stated as it is to the composition of a musical "theme and variations." If the theme is not clear the variations will be incomprehensible.

Thus do writers on art evade the problems which concern the artist in their attempt to make fallacious theories practicable. Albert C. Barnes, in *The Art in Painting*, says: "In a cubist picture, the thread of connection with individual topics or objects may be very slight, and the picture is certainly not moving because it incorporates the values of the individual thing represented. For example, it may show a violin disintegrated into many planes, all revealing partial views, seen from various angles, rendered with every degree of distortion, and recombined into a form which is plastic but not representative, and which may have a charm and an emotional force all its own. The degree of resemblance between picture and original may be so slight that, but for the title, identification would be impossible. Even when identification is made, aesthetic satisfaction may be increased little if at all."

But what charm and emotional force may there be, beyond what pattern can give, in the wreckage of forms once significant; in forms "rendered with every degree of distortion" and recombined into shapes sometimes ingenious in design, but whose newly acquired *form* is without significance? Let us recall Duchamp's "Nude Descending the Staircase"; or "Violin," by Picasso. To be told that such shapes as these works contain may be plastic but not representative only adds to the general mystification. Seldom have works of this sort third dimension and never are they anything but lines, colors, lights and shadows.

The word plastic is perhaps the most misused of all words in contemporary speech relative to artistic matters. Plastic means that which is capable of being molded: in sculpture, the sculptor's actual materials; in painting, form which has the appearance of being molded. In other words, plastic form is form which has been given, or has the appearance of having been given, a three-dimensional character. This is the simplest meaning of the word and its bearing on artistic problems is perfectly clear. There is another use of the word *plastic* which, as given by the dictionary, comes under the term *plastic element*. This is defined as "an element which contains the germ of a higher form—or which has the power to give form to matter." And there is yet another term, *plastic force*, which is defined as "the force which gives to matter a definite organic form." We can at once rule out this last definition as applicable in the case of the cubists for, in their works, any suspicion that plasticity may embody a force which would give to matter a definite organic form would be beside the mark. Definite organic form is not evident in works which are composed of "distorted," "disintegrated" fragments of forms once significant, whose past significance is demolished and whose present form we cannot understand when we see it.

We can also dismiss the first definition of *plastic*

as of form which has, simply, third dimension, or that has been given the appearance of a third dimension. It is, in itself, too direct, too simple, too obvious, to arouse intangible speculation. To give a work charm and emotional force by merely giving it third dimension is surely not the abstract artist's ambition. He must intend a higher goal. His words lead us to believe that he intends a higher goal. Therefore we surmise that this must be to embody in his forms the *plastic element* which contains the germ of a higher form. Indeed, Mr. Barnes says: "When we cannot find in a picture representation of any particular object, what it represents may be the qualities which all particular objects share, such as color, extensity, solidity, movement, rhythm, etc. All particular things have these qualities; hence, what serves, so to speak, as a paradigm of the visible essence of all things may hold in solution the emotions which individual things provoke in a more highly specialized form. It may give us a realizing sense of space, of externality, of colorfulness, of mobility and along with these a distillation of the feelings which spacious, colorful, moving objects provide." Still more picturesquely Mr. Barnes sums it up thus: "The cubists are interested not in the qualities which distinguish, let us say, an apple as an apple, or a woman as a woman, but in the qualities which are common to both as parts of the visible universe."

Paradigms of the visible essences of all things, distillations of apples, women, violins, which "may" be represented by forms which are "plastic but not representative." May be, but are they? Elucidation in chemical terms or by musical illustration of the abstract artist's intentions is all equally beside the point. It does not cause the form itself to become a visual realization of the artist's intention.

Truth frequently seems paradoxical, inconsistent and fantastic. It is reputed to be stranger than fiction; but it would seem even stranger than this, for the writer on abstract art has not even guessed at it, possibly because it is very much simpler than he suspects: those qualities common to all things in the visible universe, "color, extensity, solidity, movement, etc.," become *qualities* only as they are visualized through the medium of individual things—through the medium of particular form. Mr. Barnes' and Miss Allen's writings serve only to illustrate why it is that the works of the cubists are monuments to human credulity and the folly of words.

The world has been told repeatedly that Cubism was originally inspired by the influence of Cézanne— his works and his theories. It is said that the letter to Émile Bernard containing the phrase about the cylinder, the sphere, the cone, published in 1907, a year after Cézanne's death, led the Cubists, Braque and Picasso, to "geometrize, to reduce to fundamental geometric forms the disorder of nature," as Alfred H. Barr has it. Again there is a story that Cubism began, quite simply, when Picasso exhibited his picture of packing cases called "Portrait of My Father"; that this picture was freely imitated and, with all the clever talk it stimulated, launched Cubism on its course. However it may all have come about, the abstract artist, as we have been told many times, has been, and still says he is engaged upon a search for essential, or fundamental, form in his works.

Now, exact geometrical forms are fundamental forms. In the arts they are forms used for generalizing particular form, i.e., for reducing highly complex forms to their lowest, or, let us rather say, their simplest, terms. They are the only abstract forms which state form and content inevitably as one and the same. These forms have served for many centuries, as they serve today, as a foundation for design, but in themselves they have been found insufficient to satisfy the artist's demands as a means of expression. Forms generalized on true mathematical principles, as we see them in Greek and Egyptian works, for instance, serve a necessary end as an outline for the artist's work—a plan for his procedure. But as an end to be pursued in themselves, even in a search for the fundamental character of form, they are too limited to convey those other and equally important abstract qualities which make a work of art. Apart from occasional obvious patterns such as would do well in linoleum designs, the Cubists' quasi-geometrical shapes do not appear to be based on true forms. Not only are they not really geometrical forms, they are so *amorphous* that they cannot be called abstractions in the sense of generalizations of form. As examples of researches in the fundamental character of form they are only laughable. They have no authority, they convey no sense of order nor of the inevitable as we have these qualities in the works of the older masters or in many of the works of Cézanne. We feel, on the contrary, that the Cubists' forms were invented as they were for no particular reason—that they might have been just as well some other way.

As works of art seem at all times to have inspired writers with at least some proportion of irrelevant, and sometimes even inept, thoughts, it is not surprising that "abstract" works should do so in much higher proportion. In fact it is practically impossible to find any writing in their behalf which is relevant, not to say intelligible. In Mr. Barr's book, *Cubism and Abstract Art*, which is an earnest endeavor to rationalize the abstractionists, there is, on page 101, an analysis by one Harriet Janis of Picasso's "The Painter and His Model," opposite the illustration of this work. This analysis, as an eminent critic has well said, shows "what happens when some one tries to validate the abstractionist." The analysis, of which we quote only a few lines, runs thus: "By a constant recession of front planes and equally forceful advance of rear planes, Picasso achieves a counterbalance of spatial weights producing two-dimensional equilibrium. This activity is assisted by the directional drive of the heavy black lines, through the open construction of which it may be observed . . . Picasso has avoided the deflated vitality of decorative flat pattern by transforming the three dimensions of nature into plastic elements of a new two-dimensional integration." At this moment we can do no better than join Mr. Cortissoz in saying: "On which gorgeous mouthful I can only observe with the bard 'O, wonderful, wonderful, and most wonderful wonderful! and yet again wonderful and after that out of all hooping.'" Mr. Cortissoz also suggests that we should match the picture with the analysis and, upon so doing, we can find no point at which they correspond. We should say instead that the work was an excellent illustration of what the analyst says Picasso avoided—"deflated vitality of decorative flat pattern."

Writers have become so skilled in spreading the confusion of language that the reader, bewildered, thinks his inability to understand their writings means that their sense must be profound, as must the meaning of the works about which they write. He has only to turn to the works of Picasso, Arp, Leger, for example, to see that their sense is not profound but only obscure, as obscure as the writings themselves. Had he never read these writings he would be sadly at a loss to explain the works, and the works' significance thus verbally attempted, what does it convey?

For instance, let us consider for a moment the meaning of the term *planes*, made mysterious by indiscriminate use. Planes seem elusive and difficult to define because they do not exist independently but are the flat or plane surfaces of solid forms. As it is necessary to indicate the faces of a cube in presenting that form in its solid aspect, so the artist applies the same principle to the simplification of higher forms—mountains, trees, or the human body, for example. This procedure he adopts in the early stages of his work when he suggests, or "blocks" out, his forms in what he imagines to be their essential character seen in flattened or plane surfaces. These higher forms, in the final development of his work, are curved and flowing continually into one another without demarcation; the unity of form and content achieved. Now the Cubists do not advance in their works beyond the crudest stages of such "blocking" or planning, nor do the flat shapes used by them as planes in any way indicate a higher order of form to be attained; the unity of form and content. As in nature all things have form essential to their being, so in works of art form and content must be one and the same. Those flat shapes called planes, which are only a means to an end—instruments to a higher goal—cannot stand independently as ultimate realizations of form. They can only serve as suggestions to the individual artist to guide him in the process of his work. That they may stand by themselves as ultimate realizations of form is the fallacy at the heart of the abstractionist's theory. The outer aspect of every living thing is the manifestation of inner vitality. The outer has no existence without the inner and the inner has no means of reaching fulfillment except in the outer. The same is true of that quality called form in those works by man called works of art—works of art, not of craftsmanship however skilled. And unless the artist is master of his medium his form will not convey his intention, for mastery is a sign that the inner and the outer are understood as one. Of these qualities there are none, visually realized, in the work of the abstractionists.

There is a recent English publication called *Circle* which, as its jacket informs the reader, "is an authoritative survey of one of the most active movements in modern art. Painters, sculptors, architects and writers of fourteen different nationalities have combined to give complete exposition of their ideas and practice.

The text is illustrated by photographs and plans which are in themselves a pictorial record of the actual achievements of a movement whose significance for the reconstruction of modern civilization is now for the first time made fully evident."

Let us examine a little of the evidence.

First, there is a "new concept of the world represented by the Constructive idea." And this Constructive idea in art "embraces those two fundamental elements of which Art is built up, namely, the Content and the Form. These two elements are, from the Constructive point of view, one and the same thing. It does not separate Content from Form—on the contrary, it does not see as possible their separated and independent existence. The thought that Form could have one designation and Content another cannot be incorporated in the concept of the Constructive idea. In a work of art they have to live and act as a unit, proceed in the same direction and produce the same effect. I say 'have to' because never before in art have they acted in such a way in spite of the obvious necessity of this condition. It has always been so in Art that either one or the other predominated, conditioning and predetermining the other."

It is scarcely necessary to point out to the reader that the thesis of the Constructive idea is far from being a "new concept of the world" from the artist's point of view, or that the statement that never before have form and content lived and acted as a unit in art, is without foundation. Thought so false as this reaches verbal expression only because of the desire to create an hypothesis for the explanation of works which do not explain themselves.

The writer of this chapter on the Constructive idea, N. Gabo, follows these remarkable statements with statements even more remarkable. He says: ". . . in all our previous Art concepts of the world a work of art could not have been conceived without the representation of the external aspect of the world . . . Even in those cases where the artist tried to concentrate his attention only on the inner world of his perceptions and emotions, he could not imagine the picture of this inner world without the images of the outer one. The most that he could dare in such cases was the more or less individual distortions of the external images of Nature; that is, he altered only the scale of the relations between the two worlds, always keeping to the main system of its content, *but did not attack the fact of their dependence; . . .*" [Author's italics.] Here is flagrant contradiction. N. Gabo says that it has "always been so in art that either (form or content) predominated, conditioning and predetermining the other." He then says that in all previous art concepts of the world, the artist "did not attack the fact of their dependence." In his next paragraph, N. Gabo convicts himself of tortuous thinking in a confusion of words: "The apparently ideal companionship between Form and Content in the old Art was indeed an unequal division of rights and was based on the obedience of the Form to the Content. This obedience is explained by the fact that all formalistic movements in the history of Art, whenever they appeared, never went so far as to presume the possibility of an independent existence of a work of art apart from the naturalistic content, nor to suspect that there might be a concept of the world which could reveal a Content in a Form."

There is no need of wearying the reader by pursuing further the Circle's Constructive idea. He will have seen for himself that its basic concept—that there must be unity of form and content in art—while sound in itself, is most unsoundly developed by the most inconsequential, the most fallacious kind of thinking. It is at moments like this that we particularly appeal to the layman not to fear his own judgment and, if he fails to understand such thought as is contained in these paragraphs by N. Gabo, not to lay it to his own supposed stupidity or to his lack of a knowledge of art, but to recognize it for what it is—a senseless jumble of words.

A passage from Plato's *Philebus* is often quoted and now rapidly becoming famous as support, if not as authority, for abstract art. Socrates says to Protarchus: "I do not mean by beauty of form such beauty as that of animals or pictures, which the many would suppose to be my meaning; but, understand me to mean straight lines and circles, and the plane or solid figures which are formed out of them by turning lathes and rulers and measurers of angles; for these I affirm to be not only relatively beautiful, like other things, but they are eternally and absolutely beautiful."

Socrates refers to geometry, and geometry is a part of the science of mathematics. Geometrical forms are fundamental forms, universal forms, exact forms, brought within the bounds of definition. They stand by themselves, are perfect in themselves and are therefore absolute. They serve the end of truth and unless their laws are obeyed and their purpose respected they are likely to undo the efforts of those who trifle with them by destroying any appearance of truth in their works. But because they are perfect forms their powers are also restricted—they are only a part of nature's unlimited resources—and if we are to be artists we must seek further development of our art among the many and varied means nature places at our disposal. It is well to remember that neither Socrates nor Plato was an artist and, while their point of view is true and wholly just as far as it goes, the limitations of forms "absolutely beautiful" might not cause them regret but might, on the contrary, serve to increase their intellectual satisfaction in the perfection of their argument. For an artist, on the other hand, it is necessary that he should understand those limitations, that, through understanding, he may pursue his desires for fulfillment in more complex forms—in such beauty of form "as that of animals or pictures." Instead of authority, or even support for the theory of "abstract art," Socrates' words make a mock of the twentieth-century "abstract artist's" pretensions.

The reader, for his own delectation, may imagine a conversation between Socrates, N. Gabo, Mr. Barnes, and Mr. Barr . . .

CHAPTER SEVEN

PRIMITIVE ART, CHILD ART AND THE INNOCENT EYE

MUCH has been said of the serious influences which the art of primitives and of children—that is, the children of civilized races—have had upon the non-traditional artist's works. This subject is also one in which great confusion of thought exists, and largely because the entire product of both is indiscriminately called art. While it is evident that primitive man has produced works of art, and that the gifted civilized child is occasionally capable of producing them, it does not therefore follow that everything either produces is art. This is, indeed, very far from being the case.

Primitive art, as we use the term today, embraces the drawing, painting and sculpture of the unskilled ordinary savage; those works which show skill in craftsmanship, and rare works by men whose capacity as artists has far outstripped their fellows'; who have achieved a sophisticated expression as astonishing as it is beautiful; a form as forceful in character and intention as the form of many works of the civilized periods of history (witness the paintings in the caves of Altamira); a product which may well be called art, which the contemporary artist may well set himself as an example; one, moreover, which is fully comprehensible as art and needs no verbal explanation. But this last is not the product which has influenced the contemporary artist. There is no trace in his works of thought derived from this source. It is, on the contrary, to the large majority of works of the ordinary savage, such as are most frequently seen in contemporary exhibitions, that he has turned for inspiration. Not only do these display the grotesque character, the sardonic humor of the mature but undeveloped mind of their creators, but their form is crude, elementary, and without artistic significance. These are works which have meaning only in the surroundings in which they were created. Because their form frequently appears distorted to civilized standards, it is the fashion of our day to conclude that they are profoundly expressive of essential artistic qualities, of "intrinsic meanings"; of a depth and intensity of emotion not discernible in the art of civilized peoples. Herbert Read says: "We can learn more of the essential nature of art from its earliest manifestations in primitive man (and in children) than from its intellectual elaboration in great periods of culture. For in its later stages art is overlaid by modes and manners that are not of its essence."

It is easy to generalize as Mr. Read does in his eagerness to substantiate a theory. The important works of art of any civilization—the works which make the great periods of culture—are never overlaid by modes and manners that are not of their essence. This condition occurs in the works of imitators when a civilization has run its course and has begun to deteriorate. When the art of any period weakens, "modes and manners" become overdeveloped, as if to take the place of a lost vitality. And is it about the essential nature of *art* that we learn from the large majority of works of the primitive, and from those of the civilized child? Not if we are to judge by the works of those contemporary artists who have emulated them. John Dewey, in *Art as Experience*, says: "I suppose the fetishes of the Negro sculptor were taken to be useful in the highest degree to his tribal group, more so even than spears and clothing. But now they are fine art, serving in the twentieth century to inspire renovations in arts that had grown conventional. But they are fine art only because the anonymous artist lived and experienced so fully during the process of production."

But are they truly fine art for this reason? When we think of the kind of full living and experiencing most of these "anonymous artists" had, we wonder what has become of the critical faculties of our contemporary writers. Few forms even of primitive expression are more limited and conventional than the fetish of the Negro sculptor; few forms are so crude as these, or display such elementary perceptions; few are further removed from any artistic significance.

The theory that form in contemporary non-traditional works displays a grasp of essential qualities *because* it is conceived in the same crude character as the crudest of primitive form, is one of the great absurdities in our manner of thinking. It is one of the follies of theorists to the falsity of which the history of art bears silent witness. There is purpose visible in the primitive's form even in its crudest, most elementary, state. There is no visible purpose in the contemporary non-traditional artist's crudity.

In a remarkable chapter on the sculpture of the African Negro, in his book, *Vision and Design*, Roger Fry draws a marked contrast between the Negro's art and all archaic European art—"Greek and Romanesque for instance." He says the European "statue bears traces of having been conceived as the combination of front, back, and side bas-reliefs. And this continues to make itself felt almost until the final development of the tradition. Complete plastic freedom with us seems only to come at the end of a long period, when the art has attained a high degree of representational skill and when it is generally already decadent from the point of view of imaginative significance.

"Now, the strange things about these African sculptures is that they bear, as far as I can see, no trace of this process. Without ever attaining anything like representational accuracy they have complete freedom. The sculptors seem to have no difficulty in getting away from the two-dimensional plane. The neck and torso are conceived as cylinders, not as masses with a square section. The head is conceived as a pear-shaped mass. It is conceived as a single whole, not arrived at by approach from the mask, as with all primitive European art. The mask itself is conceived as a concave plane cut out of this otherwise perfectly unified mass."

We are asked in all solemnity to find that European sculpture from the archaic period "almost until the final development of the tradition" bears traces of having been conceived from a two-dimensional point of view: that is, built up of a combination of "front, back and side bas-reliefs," or as "masses with a square section"—whatever that may mean. Not only can we find no traces of these strange characteristics in European sculpture but we find no sense in Roger Fry's phrases. They are so much abracadabra. We agree that the necks and torsos of African sculptures are frequently conceived as cylinders; this is quite plain in African works. But if cylinders exemplify complete plastic freedom, why should we not choose the stove-pipe as the highest example of three-dimensional or plastic form? Indeed, upon only a brief survey of contemporary painting and sculpture it would appear that we do. But surely this is a limited conception of plastic form rather than a conception denoting freedom.

There is much more of a similar nature in this chapter on the African Negro which we recommend the reader to study. But its last paragraph we quote here. "It is curious that a people who produced such great artists did not produce a culture in our sense of the word. This shows that two factors are necessary to produce the cultures which distinguish civilized peoples. There must be, of course, the creative artist, but there must also be the power of conscious critical appreciation and comparison. If we imagined such an apparatus of critical appreciation as the Chinese have possessed from the earliest times applied to this Negro art, we should have no difficulty in recognizing its singular beauty. We should never have been tempted to regard it as savage or unrefined."

We wonder. We wonder also how it happens that if civilized races have been given powers of conscious critical appreciation and comparison, our writers on art have not put them to better use.

It is worthy of note, even at the risk of undue repetition, that in the rare instances where a consideration of form has entered the works of primitive man, he has chosen to emphasize it as does the European. That is to say, wherever his works display a preoccupation with formal expression, an understanding of "planes," they bear a striking resemblance in character to the art of the European. Wherever art enters the works of any race, the conception of form is always the same, however the style of expression may differ. This conception lies in the use of representational form as a medium, not to describe objects as our theorists persist in stating, but to present the artist's visualized idea so that it may be recognizable to the beholder, in its own purposeful language.

As we examine the various theories presented by twentieth-century non-traditional artists and by those who write about their works, we are increasingly impressed by their need to account, in some fashion, for what appears to be their evasion of the problems presented by representational form as the artist's natural medium of expression. To master such form requires more than mere skill in the representation of objects. It requires the genius which can make use of it as a means to an end—the genius which masters emotion and intellect.

Of the works of children and primitive peoples,

Mary Cecil Allen says: "The vital quality of primitive art lies in what the pattern stands for, not in the pattern itself. This is why child art has been the inspiration of the modern Renaissance. The child is absorbed in his vision, his intention, and, however bold and exciting the shapes may be which he invents to express his thought on paper, the shapes are not the important things to him. He has something to say, and this underlying meaning so far from being a literary weakness extraneous to the artistic worth of his picture, is the very life of it."

But one might inquire if the vital quality of the child's product does not lie in the pattern itself, wherein does it lie? If it is not in the pattern or form, how can it be seen and felt as the very life of his picture? Miss Allen continues to confuse the issue. She says: "When a child draws an angry man's head as an immense irregular oval with circular eyes, a square mouth, and makes a disconnected scribble at the top of the paper, which he calls anger, he is doing exactly the same thing as the savage who combines crude symbols in a devil mask. Both are engaged in a highly abstract and personal creation.

"The fact must also be faced that, to a certain extent, the results will be a secret cipher. Only those who naturally tend to associate the same chain of ideas in somewhat the same order will be able to read this personal language of art with ease. It is a noticeable fact that children are not particularly interested in the drawings of other children, and for a very curious reason. It is really because they do not understand them. Each child is using such a personal cipher—that it will nearly always be found necessary for one child to interpret his picture to another in words."

Precisely so. The child's shapes are not symbols or ciphers, nor is his "underlying meaning" the very life of his picture; therefore he necessarily resorts to words to explain his intentions. Through all the muddle Miss Allen stumbles upon the great secret without, apparently, being aware that she has disclosed it. But if the child's shapes are neither symbols nor ciphers the shapes the primitive uses are, on the contrary, often symbols, signs, whose particular meaning is shared by himself and his fellows. When his forms are not symbolic or starkly representational, they are often highly conventionalized to serve a particular purpose. His works leave us in little doubt as to what was in his mind. But the works of children rarely tell us anything and it becomes necessary to explain them in words.

In writings of the kind we have been examining there is a great deal made of something called the "innocent eye." Herbert Read tells us, for example, that the works of Matisse "have been compared, not unreasonably with children's drawings. Because in both you have the same pre-logical vision, the same delight of the innocent eye." But the innocent eye, in the mature artist, is a figment of the theorist's imagination. No one whose mind has developed normally or who possesses even the rudiments of an education—and it is scarcely possible to live in the present-day world without some contact with its usages—can have an innocent eye or a pre-logical vision. In the case of M. Matisse this is pre-eminently so. He served a long and arduous apprenticeship as a copyist of traditional works. Thomas Craven, in *Modern Art*, gives an entertaining account of his early career. "Matisse, however, was no ordinary copyist. Working daily in the museums, he kept his wits about him, studied the styles and methods of the men of every period, and acquired extensive knowledge of the technical history of art. But it was true, as he said, that he painted just as every one else painted, and he was very unhappy. He felt that he was not honest with himself, that his diligence was getting him nowhere . . . that what he was doing had no connection with the life of his own age. Whereupon a change came over him. Slowly, and with the caution for which he is famous, he moved toward the stormy centers of radicalism. . . . He joined the Impressionists. . . . He went into divisionism. . . . He applied his inventive talent to Cézanne;

then to Gauguin and Van Gogh; and from Van Gogh he hurried to Negro sculpture and the flat designs of the Orientals. From these sources he compiled an elliptical style of expression which gained him the derisive title of 'Leader of the Pack of Wild Animals'; but which, after the unpleasant notoriety had died down, rewarded him with a large and steady income." Matisse has been a shrewd observer of human nature, but it has not gained him either a pre-logical vision or an innocent eye.

Matisse is an artist who has sought in some way to develop a style of his own out of the vision of others. An artist who seeks consciously to originate a style will never be noted for originality. Original style is not acquired. It is the result of clarity of mind in expressing a particular way of seeing. If a painter has no style of his own it is either because what he sees and feels is not clear enough or strong enough within his own mind to withstand the doubts and uncertainties that come to him as they come to all artists, or because what he sees is seen as others before him have seen it.

The type of mind which caused Matisse to copy so ably many years ago is still the type of mind displayed in his works today. He is the able imitator who, for lack of those qualities which go to make the original creative artist, has most shrewdly relied upon verbal explanation of what he sees and feels to convey his intention. His works are unconvincing as examples of the painter's art.

We have said that explanations of the non-traditional artist's works are made necessary because he evades the problems which representational form, as the natural means of expression, creates for him. Perhaps they arise from another need as well—the bitter necessity to escape the consciousness of mediocre performance in its use. To the artist of shrewd intelligence there is nothing more condemning than the realization that his ability is no more than commonplace. And the fact remains, no matter how he attempts to evade it, that the manner in which he makes use of representational form is the measure of his capacity as an artist; that unless he masters it, unless he rises above its difficulties, his intentions are likely to be misunderstood.

We have seen how, in Cézanne's case, intensity of purpose gave his works the character of sincerity, but also how his inability to master representational form led to the most extravagant theorizings by the outside world as to his intentions. Even so able a writer as Lionello Venturi, who has said in his book on Cézanne that the common belief that Cézanne prepared the basis for the movement in painting away from realistic representation toward abstraction is contradicted by both Cézanne's works and his words, has fallen for the popular theory that Cézanne was a rebel in the face of tradition, that his heroic fight was not against nature but against prejudice. He says that in common with Titian and Velasquez, Cézanne was a robust executant before being an "artist authentique," and that the belief that he could not realize because he had not learned what was taught in the schools was a ridiculous and tragic error. M. Venturi goes even further and says, in a comparison of Cézanne's early and later drawings, that the uncertainties and deformations which we see in the latter occur because he abandoned the old system and had not yet mastered the new—"an entire transformation of lines, of light and of shade, of values." In Cézanne's singularly defective work, the "Portrait of Ambroise Vollard," M. Venturi says that there appears "the wind of passion which bore Cézanne upon the course of his later years in which the painter manifests himself in the somber hues, in the air of grave preoccupation and severe expression of the face." Thus may a writer of exceptional knowledge and understanding write many words about an artist's works which serve only the cause of mystification.

Much the same sort of extravagant verbal fancies are composed in explanation of the works of Cézanne's self-styled followers led by Picasso, Matisse, Braque, which display none of Cézanne's sincerity or intensity of purpose to urge the theorist to further understanding of their intentions. But words will not in the end conceal the commonplace any more than they will elucidate unintelligibility in the use of the artist's medium. For instance, it is said that Picasso can draw very well when he pleases. By this is meant that he can make intelligible use of representational form as it is to be seen in his line drawings. Now this we do not doubt, but it is much more important to know in what manner he draws than that he can draw well. That is, we should ask, does his drawing show sensibility, distinction in choice of emphasis, subtlety of understanding in the use of his medium, so that the sum of these qualities presents a consistent whole, whether summary in execution or carried far toward a finish, that we may see the artist's intention realized; or, is his drawing simply "good drawing," well executed in a commonplace manner? It is also said that Picasso advocates a "return to Ingres." Let us therefore compare his drawings with those of Ingres, and we shall see plainly that they are remarkable only for their commonplace conception and manner of execution.

When words and phrases have been repeatedly used over a long period of time they become accepted and believed in as emanating from a source of wisdom. Whether or not they have any real meaning, either in themselves or in application to works of art, becomes unimportant, and few minds incline to trouble about their sense. The expression "innocent eye" is a figure of speech. Some say the Impressionists originated it, others that their followers, the Post-Impressionists, made enthusiastic use of it. However this may be, if the matter were to be given real thought it could readily be seen that the term was coined to emphasize the desire on the part of thinking painters to make of their senses—and their color sense in particular—a keen instrument of vision by close observation of nature and analysis of what they saw, unprejudiced by theory. But that there was innocence in the ordinary sense of the word, of guilelessness or ignorance, or a lack of conscious effort to think or make logical every step in their procedure, was far from being the case. So far, indeed, that many ran afoul of the very shoals they sought to avoid—theoretical formulae. When we hear about the innocent eye, then, in the search for essential form in the formless works of the leaders of twentieth-century cults, we may know we are no longer seeing with our eyes, but are listening with our ears; and that without great thought as to what it is to which we are listening.

It seems not to occur to artists or to writers on art that the attempt on the part of mature persons to be naïve and simple, to see innocently, means the inevitable negation of naïveté, simplicity and innocence; nor that to attempt to see with the vision of a child in the manner of many of our contemporary artists can result in anything other than works which are counterfeit; which are not creative but imitative; which lack conviction because they are not genuine, and which therefore cannot speak for themselves but must be spoken for.

CHAPTER EIGHT

SCIENCE AND MYSTIFICATION

HAVING examined the comparatively concrete influences of primitive and child art let us consider some of the consequences to art of the science of psychology and the various philosophies. This will, perforce, be a limited examination because of the inexhaustible character of these subjects. It can, therefore, only be suggested in these pages.

We noted earlier that the attitude of mind of the non-traditional twentieth-century artist appears to be very different from that of Cézanne and his contemporaries, and from that of artists throughout history; that his is an attitude of mind in which conscious self-expression is the important factor, in which he attempts to nourish self-expression with self-knowledge. Many people believe that psychological investigation in the field of art has resulted in a scientific approach, not only to a greater understanding of art, but to a greater understanding by the artist of himself.

In this age much passes for science, however, which

is not science even in the broadest sense of the word, synonymous with learning or knowledge. In his Harveian Oration Sir Henry Dale draws a clear and fine distinction between the two kinds of learning, that which is true knowledge and that which is speculative. He says: "To us it may seem now to be a platitude that science advances by experiment and by direct appeal to nature, rather than by disputation about what others have observed or we ourselves have thought and believed. Yet, as Harvey seems to have foreseen, all of us . . . need still to be reminded of this now familiar truth. The winning of real knowledge by experiment is slow and laborious and exacts a stern discipline, while speculation offers an easy invitation to the ingenious mind. Theories we must have to give system to our facts and direction to our experiments; and the temptation is ever present—to the eager experimenter, even more, perhaps, than to the quiet observer—to press new facts into the framework of a plausible theory and to distrust and to disparage those which refuse to fit easily into a fancied picture. We stand all in daily need of Harvey's exhortation, to approach nature with a clear vision and alert attention, so that we may receive her teaching with free and humble minds."

The kind of thought so far reviewed in these pages is not the kind that comes from a knowledge of things at first hand. It comes instead from the storehouse of the acquisitive mind which collects information from any source and attempts to relate a few facts and much conjecture, pressing all together, without distinction, into a "framework of plausible theory," applying the "science" thus achieved here and there in pleasing phraseology. Hypotheses thus assembled are deceptive because they are not wholly true. They inspire methods of thought about things which are outside the character of those things. We shall see if the "scientific" thought of our day upon matters of art is not of this order.

We learn, for example, that ". . . in studying art, man is seeking to know himself through the mirror of his own mind." Now is this, in truth, the study of art? The phrase occurs in the introduction, written by Philip Youtz, to a book called *Scientific Method in Aesthetics* by Thomas Munro, and we quote it here because it sums up, briefly, the new attitude toward art. The book itself says that "Logical analysis and observation of the regularities in aesthetic experience are necessary to scientific understanding," but how such regularities are to be classified, even by means of the paraphernalia of modern methods of investigation, appears uncertain. Such investigation aims "not at directing the courses of intuitive impulse, but at freeing it to seek its own paths of adventure and growth, by harmonizing unwonted conflicts, and dissolving the routines of mechanical habit." And yet in a discreet phrase quite early in the book the author says: "If the critic were to transfer his attention too much to his own responses, most of them would immediately cease to operate; self-consciousness would stifle them." If this is true of the critic, how much more true must it be of the creator!

Nevertheless, those who have dedicated themselves to the science of art in the attempt to set free intuitive impulse by harmonizing unwonted conflicts, or by other means equally nebulous, contend cheerfully that their efforts to define aesthetic experience are not intended to make men into artists. Indeed no, under no circumstances should they be suspected of such presumption! When we inquire to what purpose, then, they teach the results of their investigations, they answer: to aid the artist in an understanding of his own functions and the nature of his works; to bring sanity and fresh observation to his approach to art. In their optimism they forget that the results of their investigations stifle, and by their own admission, the very impulses they seek to liberate. They forget that in the making of a work of art it is necessary that the artist shall be an instrument for his performance; that what he does shall convey his intention through the power of his agency. When the artist's attention is directed upon himself, when he seeks to know himself through the mirror of his own mind, he is no longer an instrument for such performance but becomes an object, often pitiful, of speculation and doubt. However sincere his intentions may be his works will not have artistic sincerity, springing from so false an attitude.

But let us turn from the creator, for a moment, to consider the case of the observer, for these things concern him almost as much as they do the creator. Let us see what so-called scientific investigation into methods of appreciation and criticism by writers on art may do for him. In the *Art of Renoir*, Albert C. Barnes and Violette de Mazia write thus in concert: "Science . . . by excluding the individual's whims and fancies from the determination of what objectively exists, has made the physical world infinitely more amenable to the individual's enlightened purposes. The satisfactions denied him have been imaginary, those provided have been real." It is Mr. Barnes' belief that the "possibilities inherent in a painting reveal themselves to the untutored eye as little as do those of a piece of coal" and that to appreciate art "requires a grasp of the artist's specific purpose." To enlighten the observer he analyzes a number of Renoir's paintings, each with a paragraph confined to its description. We choose one paragraph at random, which runs thus: "The individual colors in 'Woman in Landscape'—greens, yellows, reds, lavenders, blues —are juicy, luscious, rich, deep and glowing, and so, too, is the pervasive multicolored glow of the suffusion. A vast number of small brush strokes form an all-over pattern of color-light units and add sparkle to the general effulgent glow. The individual brush strokes, by their relationships in color and tone, appear to interpenetrate in deep space, and thus make up a pattern which forms an integral part of the structure of solid color-volumes."

Mr. Barnes admits the difficulties. He says that "learning to see pictures as records of enriched experience is of necessity slow, even when interest is genuine and application wholehearted." But he says that "progress has begun when the beholder, pausing for reflection, becomes conscious that his senses are feeding upon the objective traits of the painting, that the nutriment furnished is stirring his imagination, and a feeling of warmth pervades his whole organism." After reading Mr. Barnes' multicolored descriptions of Renoir's works, and of what are presumably his own sensations in their presence, we not only fail to be impressed by his presentation of Renoir's specific purpose, but are forced to conclude that his "science" has failed of its mission in "excluding the individual's whims and fancies from the determination of what objectively exists." Mr. Barnes is undismayed, or possibly he is simply spellbound by the sound of his own words, for he says that from the intelligent use of objective method such as his "may be expected a personal response as completely relevant to the work of art as are the judgments of a chemist or biologist to the processes of the physical world." Thus he tells the reader that "often in Renoir these infinitely varied and intricately intertwined series of rhythms bear striking similarity of quality, extending at times to a close correspondence in structure, to the rhythmic sequence of themes and variations in Beethoven's symphonies. This kinship can be readily perceived by the trained observer tracing with his finger the rhythms in Renoir's 'Noirmoutier,' for example, as he listens to the second movement of Beethoven's fifth symphony. In both the painting and the music the rhythmic movement, a swinging lilt, is extremely powerful, colorful; if picked up at any point in its course, it develops constantly in variety of content and in mode of expression; each addition to the prevailing rhythm punctuates the basic underlying movement with refreshing throbs of new meaningful units. It is a powerful all-pervasive rhythmic surge that stirs the percipients' whole personality to sympathetic vibration." And this is science: a mixture compounded of words, music, and painting! We picture future generations of art students attending concerts with photograph albums of their favorite paintings under their arms. Indeed we see more than this; we think we begin to understand why many people hold that art is an escape from life, a garden of illusions in which the artist walks, living amongst his sensations as in a dream. Is the picture-lover truly to acquire a knowledge of the artist's specific purpose, to develop a response as completely relevant to his works as are the judgments of a chemist or biologist to the processes of the physical world, from such pompous blowings as this? Such a false attempt as Mr. Barnes has made to relate the arts to one another and to science would be considered by any artist, musician or scientist worthy the name, merely the most arrant nonsense.

But we have not yet seen the full flower of Mr. Barnes' scientific thought. In his book, *The Art in Painting*, we find the following truly remarkable analysis. In the chapter on the Sienese tradition he says of the works of Duccio, who lived in the thirteenth and fourteenth centuries: ". . . the usual Sienese stress upon psychological states, especially sweet sentimentality, becomes submerged in a form which claims greater attention because of its greater plastic quality. The set, doleful expressions, the static character of his figures are well embodied in patterns made up of color, line, light and shadow. The idea of the Byzantine color-compartments is maintained but it becomes more generalized, and the color is well modulated with light to give a feeling of reality, though slight, to fabrics. Color-distortions are noted in the green faces, relieved by sharp contrast of pink as the highlight on cheeks. Faces are sometimes of a blackish gray, with more red in highlights on cheeks, nose and lips, making very patterned units. The color is usually rich with a tendency to juiciness. . . ."

Now, were Duccio and the painters of his time, as also many painters from his day to ours, to come to life today, their disillusionment and sorrow in beholding the state of many of their works would be no less than tragic. And the tragedy would be deepened if they read accounts of their works as fatuous as this just quoted. It is ever the artist's sad lot to know that colors change and even vanish with the course of time. In the days of the early Italian painters green earth, an easily procured pigment, was extensively used as underpainting, particularly for the painting of flesh. Over this ground the pink tints were applied in varying thicknesses in the final touches. For these pink tints vermilions and other reds were used. Translucent pigments called "lakes" were also known in these times, but because of their fugitive character when exposed to the air were unreliable. Lakes and vermilions are both subject to change according to the methods and circumstances of their use, the lakes often disappearing altogether and the vermilions sometimes turning blackish-gray. The underpainting of green earth, on the contrary, proved permanent. Where the pink tints were most thinly applied the passage of time (and frequently the ruinous attentions of picture cleaners and restorers) has caused them to disappear, sometimes entirely, leaving the green earth exposed. There can be but one explanation for the "green with pink or red highlights on cheeks," or the "blackish-gray" faces of Duccio's paintings, and that explanation is not color-distortion by the artist. Similar conditions have prevailed all through the history of painting and the scientific reasons for them are so well known that there is no excuse for such misinterpretation.

Whichever way we turn, the ultimate result of investigation into the mind, and what we like to call the soul of the artist, whether by such "scientific" methods as Mr. Barnes employs or those of the "aesthetician" who has studied psychology and the philosophies, is always the same—it ends in descriptive verbal fancies, sometimes picturesque, more often absurd, nearly always irrelevant. True science, on the other hand, as we have just seen, may always render the artist the greatest service toward an understanding of his material problems.

Let us now see what theories of philosophy may do for the lover of art who desires to understand the artist's product. We know that towards the end of the eighteenth century there arose an ever spreading tide of philosophical writing which continued throughout the nineteenth century and has greatly influenced the formation of the subjective, or introspective, point of view so greatly the vogue in our day. Here again we cannot possibly undertake to penetrate all that has been said, but it is interesting to trace certain theories of undoubted fascination, if not to their source, at least a little way into their past history. Among these one stands out particularly and is met with on every hand today: the theory that the artist expresses in his works the spirit of the time in which he lives. Analysis of this subject, ingeniously developed and expounded, brings certain thought to light. Before we pursue this thought as we find it applied in our own day to contemporary works, let us see how John Dewey, in *Art as Experience*, applies it in his presentation of the great period in Greek art of the fifth century B.C.

"By common consent, the Parthenon is a great work of art. Yet it has aesthetic standing only as the work becomes an experience for a human being. And, if one is to go beyond personal enjoyment into the formation of theory about that large republic of art of which the building is one member, one has to be willing at some point in his reflections to turn from it to the bustling, arguing, acutely sensitive Athenian citizens, with civic sense identified with a civic religion, of whose experience the temple was an expression, and who built it not as a work of art, but as a civic commemoration. The turning to them is as human beings who had needs that were a demand for the building and that were carried to fulfilment in it; it is not an examination such as might be carried on by a sociologist in search for material relevant to his purpose. The one who sets out to theorize about the aesthetic experience embodied in the Parthenon must realize in thought what the people into whose lives it entered had in common, as creators and as those who were satisfied with it, with people in our own homes and in our own streets."

From this paragraph we form a picture of the citizens of Athens, bustling, arguing, acutely sensitive, expressing the spirit of their time, of all that was most important in their lives, in the building of the Parthenon; and we conclude that, as a work of art, the building was the happy outcome of their experience. But, in considering the Parthenon as a work of art, how do we see that experience expressed? How are we to see in it the needs which demanded the building and were brought to fulfillment in it? For answer let us first refer to history.

Long before the building of the Parthenon, Greek architects had borrowed from the ancient Egyptians the form in which they built their temples. Breasted, in *Ancient Times,** gives us certain information: "At no other time before or since were so many temples erected as in the Greek world in the Age of the Tyrants. [Toward the end of the sixth century B.C.] In Sicily and southern Italy a number of the noble temples of this age still stand to display to us the beauty and simplicity of Greek architecture when it was still at an undeveloped stage. Instead of the wooden posts of the Age of the Nobles [about 750 or 700 B.C.] these temples were surrounded by lines of plain stone columns (colonnades) in a style which we call Doric. Although the architects of the Tyrants borrowed the idea and the *form* of these colonnades from Egypt, they improved them until they made them the most beautiful columns ever designed by early architects. Like those on the Nile, these Greek temples were painted in bright colors." Breasted also says that the earliest form of stone column was a fluted shaft "closely resembling the simplest form which we found in Egypt, dating nearly 3000 B.C. Not only the whole idea of a rhythmic row of piers but also the form of each shaft was thus taken by the Greeks from Egypt." Over the course of centuries the Greeks brought their architecture to a point of perfection. In the fifth century B.C. under the leadership

* Permission of the publishers, Ginn and Company.

of Pericles, Greek civilization in Athens rose to glorious heights. But while public buildings were built of stone and marble, the citizens of Athens were still living as they had lived for many a year before. In the chapter on "Athens in the Age of Pericles" Breasted writes that "there were still no beautiful houses anywhere in Europe such as we found on the Nile. The one story front of even a wealthy man's house was simply a blank wall, usually of sundried brick, rarely of broken stone or masonry. Often without any windows, it showed no other opening than the door, but a house of two stories might have a small window or two in the upper story . . . This Greek house lacked all conveniences. The chimney was little better than a hole in the roof . . ." The streets of Athens were narrow, crooked lanes "winding between the bare mudbrick walls of the low houses standing wall to wall. There was no pavement nor any sidewalk . . . All household rubbish and garbage was thrown directly into the street, and there was no system of sewage." Athenian life, lived mostly out of doors, was simple and unpretentious. Pericles, great statesman and patron of the arts, undertook to restore to Athens the beauty of her public monuments destroyed in war. His new building plans were brought before the assembly of the people who voted their adoption with enthusiasm in spite of the immense outlay of public funds which they required. Every citizen thus had a voice in the creation of the new beauty which came to Athens. At the instigation of Pericles, and at the hands of Ictinus the architect, Phidias the sculptor, and the many other artists and artisans who worked at their direction, the Parthenon rose into being. Years passed, but war came once again to Athens and there were signs that the power of Pericles was waning. Before long he lost control and was tried and fined for mis-appropriation of funds. The absence of his steadying hand and powerful leadership was at once felt by the people. They realized their helplessness and turning to him again they elected him Strategus, but he soon afterwards died of the plague. There was no one to take his place and the management of Athenian affairs fell into confusion.

Professor Dewey writes about art as experience. Beyond doubt he knows what facts history discloses, but he leaves the reader with the impression that the art of the Parthenon was the result of the Athenian citizen's civic pride and religious experience, to the exclusion, apparently, of any mention of the building's architect, artists and craftsmen; or of the genius of Pericles, "a thoroughly modern man," a great statesman and patron of the arts, whose vision of a glorious Athens gave these particular men the opportunity to exercise their highly exceptional artistic gifts. As citizens of Athens, all were doubtless swayed by a common enthusiasm for their enterprise, but had the building of the Parthenon been left to the "bustling arguing" Athenian citizen without the leadership of genius, it is highly questionable whether such a building would ever have arisen for all his "acutely sensitive" disposition. Nor does Professor Dewey even suggest that the highly specialized and at the same time infinitely wider "experience" of such a man as Ictinus was the experience capable of actually bringing the Parthenon into being and making it a work of art. Citizens of all times—the "people in our own homes and in our own streets"—are genuine lovers of the arts, but have they at any time succeeded in producing art without the citizen whose special gifts have enabled him to visualize an experience which they themselves could not have visualized?

The artist is apt to be considered a curious individual by the layman—one who excites speculative thought. That he belongs to his own time—even in the rare instances when he is said to be ahead of it—and springs from the same earthly sources as his non-artist fellows, is a commonplace fact that should be obvious. But in the past there has been so much written about his special characteristics, as though he were a being apart from his surroundings, that writers must now lean equally far to the other side of balanced thought in theorizing about him as a product of his environment. Perhaps the day will come when the writer on art will find himself a better occupation than trying to account for the artist and his works in far-fetched theory—something to help him find his balance and bring him greater wisdom. But then few books on art would be written, indeed!

Having endeavored to present to the reader what few facts there are to be found in this confusing wilderness of words, there remains the question, how are we to see, in the Parthenon, those *needs* of the Athenian citizen that were a demand for the building and were brought to fulfillment in it? That is to say, taking the Parthenon as a work of art, an example of visually realized form, wherein does it express the spirit of its time? The question is almost unanswerable. But this much we may venture: that in it we see one kind of beauty brought to perfection, a beauty in which the same kind of vision is expressed as in other periods where art has flourished; that is, that beauty that comes through the power of those rarely gifted few to seize upon the essential character of nature's forms and to mold it to their purpose. By this means do we know that a civilization has reached great heights, that a race has produced men of highly developed minds and gifts, the flowers of its soil, rivaled only by those of other civilizations at their height.

Whether or not a greater art is produced when the citizen shares in its production, if only rather indirectly by voting funds and creating an atmosphere of enthusiasm, it is impossible to say. The highest art has come into being in the most diverse circumstances.

It is given to few to understand the times in which they live. But history provides the key to a knowledge of earlier times by making comparison possible. In France, in the middle of the nineteenth century, there lived a man, philosopher, historian and critic, named Hippolyte Adolphe Taine. His lectures delivered before the École des Beaux Arts not only form a thorough treatise on all aspects of imitation in the visual arts, but are a masterly exposition of his theory that to understand a work of art one must have an exact knowledge of the general state of the spirit (mind and manners) of the people and the time to which it belongs. He expounds also the idea of the interpretation of the essential character of objects, tracing it through to the source from which it springs in life itself. That which makes an artist, he says, is the habit of mind of imitating these important aspects, these essential characters. While others see only part, he seizes the spirit of the whole.

Taine's thesis, undoubtedly sound as applied by the historian and critic to his particular needs, has in our day been misconstrued. To see art as the expression of a time-spirit is not necessarily to see it *as art*. Failing in just this respect, that is, to consider our contemporary works first as art, our contemporary writers and many of our artists are trying with might and main to explain them by analysis of the spirit of their own time. They not only try to explain them thus, but are also occupied in a conscious attempt to endow painting, sculpture and architecture with qualities that shall express the spirit of their time. In this they are assisted by much reading of philosophical works and a little modern psychology, hastily consumed, poorly assimilated and returned to view in their chosen medium.

But how shall we express, knowingly, in our works of art, that which *is* the spirit of our age? For there exists the belief that somehow, consciously, the artist must incorporate in his works some quality that shall pass as a presentation of it. If this is so, it must then be understood that that quality must be a quality of his art and not merely one of the many hallmarks of place and time inevitable in all works, *good or bad*, which essentially concern their subject. These are matters for wider consideration than are being given them today by writers and artists alike.

The qualities which place works in the category of an art must be evident in their style and substance, regardless of their subject matter. And, conversely, works based upon particularly chosen subjects are not necessarily works of art because of the subjects of which they treat. We are today, however, very much by way of thinking that subjects which would seem to depict the spirit of our time do cause our works to qualify as works of art merely because of this.

In the third and fourth decades of our century many artists have turned away from the so-called abstract styles of painting to a style called "realistic" which, they consider, shows a simplified rendering of form; a style the simplicity of which is believed to efface the mechanics of art and to convey a more immediate sense of reality; a style which more readily interprets the more profound, more analytic attitude of our day.

As we have been asked to see in the Parthenon evidence of the spirit of the Athenian citizen of the fifth century B.C., so let us consider what may be the spirit of our own times as conveyed by contemporary works. In examining their style regardless of their subject matter we note, instead of simplified form, an exceptional complexity of form, both in the picture-design as a whole and in the forms of which it is composed. We note also that the first rarely shows selection, and that the latter appear redundant and maladroit. The ovoid, tubular, or starkly angular presentations of familiar shapes do not necessarily show form reduced to its most significant, expressive character; they are, on the contrary, most usually characterless formulae, badly executed, without vitality or conviction. In such manner we see depicted a great variety of subjects which we associate with the history of the human race: agriculture, industry, prosperity and riches; discontent, injustice, poverty; war, revolution and the brotherhood of man; and the more direct renderings of landscape and the human figure for their own intrinsic worth, all caparisoned in twentieth-century fashion. Contemporary paraphernalia and historic subject matter as combined in contemporary works present at one and the same time an effect of physical lifelessness and mental disturbance, of style and subject matter which have combined without producing the substance and the spirit of an art, without producing a united whole, an appearance of truth.

Of such aspect are the works in question. But the external character of a work must be significant of its spirit, or how shall we reconcile what both writer and artist say the artist presents with what we see—or, let us rather say, with what we do not see? If the form is without sensibility wherein may we perceive the spirit?

To illustrate this point we may cite the murals of Diego Rivera—a painter of great energy and capacity whose design, contrary to that of most of his contemporaries, is most ably chosen for pictorial effect, but whose form fails to support his design because it falls between the representational and the so-called realistic, conventionalized tubular-angular-ovoid styles of today, thus producing an effect lacking in both vitality and conviction. Such form is without sensibility. It is obtrusive and does not serve the effect of the whole. When we consider Giotto's form, we find it often wooden in its naïveté, but it is never superfluous or obtrusive. The intensity of the artist's feeling appears in the true simplicity of his form and every shape serves its purpose in sustaining the whole effect.

As we find difficulty in defining the particular spirit of the Athenian citizen's day mirrored in the Parthenon, even in its beauty as a work of art, so we find the same difficulty in defining the spirit of our own time in the *art* of our contemporary works. We are even beset by a greater difficulty today for we meet with a confusion of thought and intention not to be seen in the Greek temple; a confusion imposed upon us by deformation and ugliness which purport to present reality, when *verbally* explained, more simply, more profoundly, than has hitherto been known.

But deformation and ugliness in artistic expression have no power to convey anything other than deformation and ugliness. They are unable to bring to birth the qualities which make a work of art. It is confusing in the extreme to be told that they present a simplification of form; a simplification which effaces the mechanics of art and thus liberates a more profound artistic expression. These phrases are an example of what a brilliant satirist of our day calls the "phoney profundities" of the language of art.

But what of our understanding of this actual world? Is it not true that some of us rejoice in its novelties, that many of us feel that the mere fact of being alive today is the greatest privilege, the greatest inspiration anyone may have to aid him in living and in doing; and that there are others of us, less fortunate, who feel very much the reverse: that we live in an age when humanity is displaying its darkest, most inhuman characteristics, that the rapid beat of the pulse of life spells only confusion and disorder, and is very much the reverse of inspiring?

In *The Meaning of Unintelligibility in Modern Art,* Edward F. Rothschild writes that our own age is "an age of unintelligibility, as every age must be that is so largely characterized by conflict, maladjustment and heterogeneity. . . . Art, dealing with sensory and spiritual experience, with emotions and intuitions—in other words with immeasurables and imponderables— is essentially non-verbal, indefinable, impractical, if you will: and its idiom may be nebulous, fantastic, psychic, or abstract, hence unintelligible, but this situation does not jeopardise the potential quality which is the heart of the work of art, because quality is also unintelligible. . . . Modern art has made a tremendous contribution to the realization of this point of view . . . and, in a psychic age of individualism and revolution" . . . the modern artist "embraced unintelligibility, as a sublimation of his fear of being misunderstood."

Analysis of art and the artist, if indeed this can be called analysis, can delve no further into the realm of absurdity—and this we should not like to think of as a characteristic of our time. The artist who fears misunderstanding can never produce a work of art. He who embraces unintelligibility because he fears, does not fear misunderstanding, but the detection of his weaknesses because he is thinking of himself and not of his objective—"the goal to be attained."

When the artist attempts appraisal of the characteristics of the time in which he lives with a view to their presentation in his works; when, for instance, he indulges in revolutionary sentiments as do the "social-conscious" artists of our day, he undertakes a divided task and his works inevitably show the result. No human mind can compass the diverse elements which contribute to the make-up of its surroundings. We, today, may very well be historians of the past and, through study of its art, note many characteristics of its different cultures. Nevertheless it remains questionable whether it is the art of the past in which we find these characteristics, or whether they are not rather to be found in the "modes and manners not of its essence." However this may be, to attempt appraisal of the spirit of our own time is folly, for it cannot justly be done. If we attempt to render that spirit in our art, we fail as artists; but, if we concentrate our attention upon the problems immediately concerning our art with undivided mind, we may become artists whose contribution to our own times may be important *as art.*

If "peradventure the confusion of language was the destruction of arts" as the English traveler suggested in the early seventeenth century, we have ample evidence, in this twentieth century, of its destructive power. For the confusion of language means the confusion of thought; and confusion of thought is destructive to any creative enterprise. It must be remembered that aesthetic theory is something developed largely by philosophic and analytical literary minds after the fact of creation, about which they know little or nothing—minds interested not in the making of things which are real but which are interested in theorizing about the sources from which those things may spring. Those who have wisdom, when questioned on the subjects of which they treat, only make answer in parables. The wise make no pretense of knowing those things of which speculative minds appear to have such certain knowledge.

We have been unsuccessful in identifying the needs of the Athenian citizen as they are said to have been brought to fulfillment in the Parthenon as a work of art, and we have been equally unsuccessful in deducing the spirit of our own times from both contemporary works of art and the writings published about them. Such works should be appraised from one standpoint only—that of art. Whatever qualities there are to be considered in addition, should be considered secondarily, mindful of their uncertain character. But this would not seem to be the case today where qualities of secondary importance are considered first, and the art last, when considered at all.

Benjamin Jowett, writing in the last half of the nineteenth century, says of Socrates: "His mind pierces through the difference of times and countries into the essential nature of man; and his words apply equally to the modern world and to the Athenians of old. Let us take a survey of the professions to which he referred and try them by his standard. . . . Is not all literature passing into criticism, just as Athenian literature in the age of Plato was degenerating into sophistry and rhetoric? We can discourse and write about poems and paintings, but we seem to have lost the gift of creating them. Can we wonder that few of them come 'sweetly from nature,' while ten thousand reviewers are engaged in dissecting them? . . . And perhaps he [Socrates] might more severely chastise some of us for trying to invent 'a new shudder' instead of bringing to birth living and healthy creations."

CHAPTER NINE

THEIR OWN TESTIMONY

IN spite of what is today considered by many people to be our highly civilized state, brought about chiefly by rapid advances in scientific thought, it would seem that human nature still retains many of its ancient characteristics. Man, who always has been, and who will doubtless continue to be, a mixture of good and evil potentialities has still an instinctive desire for order and a love of beauty. The artist has these characteristics to a highly developed degree. They are fundamental and are not lightly set aside by the fashion in taste of a day. The standard the artist's works have created in the past will, because of these innate characteristics, serve the future as it has served the past and as it still serves the present wherever the artist is engaged in his own medium and is not bemused by words. The quality which presents that standard in recognizable form, which makes the difference between the commonplace and the important in art, is one which is characteristic of man's highest achievement in the arts throughout the ages—a unity of purpose and effect.

Yet it is frequently said that there are no standards by which works of art may be judged; that art is a matter of taste, of what we like and dislike, and of the fashion of the time; that there are no facts in art and therefore there can be no basis upon which to form opinions. These are plausible statements but they are not wholly true; and, as we have seen, that which is not wholly true is frequently dangerously false.

It is a fact in art that all important works present to the observer first and above all other effects, the effect of a united whole, no matter what the subject or the manner of its presentation. In mediocre works and in the works of theorists, on the contrary, the first impression is of too evident detail; of obtrusion, or separation of the parts, characteristics which produce an impression of divided purpose, of uncertain intention, or of preoccupation with side issues. In such works the artist's form and idea are not homogeneous. These characteristics may be seen, for example, in the more extreme of the Impressionists' works (as in Monet's overcolored canvases), and in the works of the Post-Impressionists; and most particularly are they evident in the so-called abstract works of the twentieth century.

To illustrate the two kinds of effect—the one which

is homogeneous and the other which is not—let us compare Botticelli's fantasy, "The Birth of Venus," with Matisse's improvisation called "Joie de Vivre." In the first we are immediately aware of the spirited effect of the whole work. In the second we are conscious of the lines and masses which compose it. More carefully, let us look at Bellini's "St. Francis" in the Frick Collection and then at Leon Kroll's "Cape Ann" in the Metropolitan Museum, thus trying a great work and a mediocre by the standard inevitably imposed by the great. When we look into Bellini's picture we see that the bold character of his form is striking in its skilled simplicity; that its uncompromising realism radiates the highest qualities of an artist's imagination; that the scrupulous attention to detail is such as to emphasize the unity of the picture's effect—an effect so completely a whole that these definite characteristics are nowhere dominating and the result is a work of an emotional intensity perhaps unequaled in any age; an effect which tells, without need of words, all there is to tell. When we see Leon Kroll's "Cape Ann" we are instantly conscious of the work's detail—of the obtrusive character of its redundant form. The component parts of the work are not so related as to convey those rare but necessary qualities of the imagination which cause works to rise above the commonplace. They are instead seen piece by piece and the picture is, therefore, obvious without being forceful. It fails to present the effect of a united whole.

We have said that fundamental principles in the arts are few and simple, and it should here be added that essential among them are these: that the detail of a work and the means by which it is accomplished should be subordinate to the effect of the whole; that the effect of the whole should be conveyed to the observer by means of the eye, in form which is intelligible to the eye. This same thought should be applied to the color of a work, i.e., a work should have an effect of color and not be merely so many patches of different-colored paints. Furthermore, the work should convey the artist's intention, not verbally by either him or his spokesman, but realized in the artist's proper medium. It may also be observed here that the quality and the caliber of an artist's gifts will appear in his works, either to glorify him as an artist or to betray him as such, despite anything he can consciously do to enhance them.

Were it not for the intermediary between layman and artist who writes books about art, to the layman's bewilderment, the latter would have a better chance to think for himself, as would also the student of today: a better chance to pursue further his interest in art and, by independent observation and study of the artist's works (for which nowadays he has opportunity in

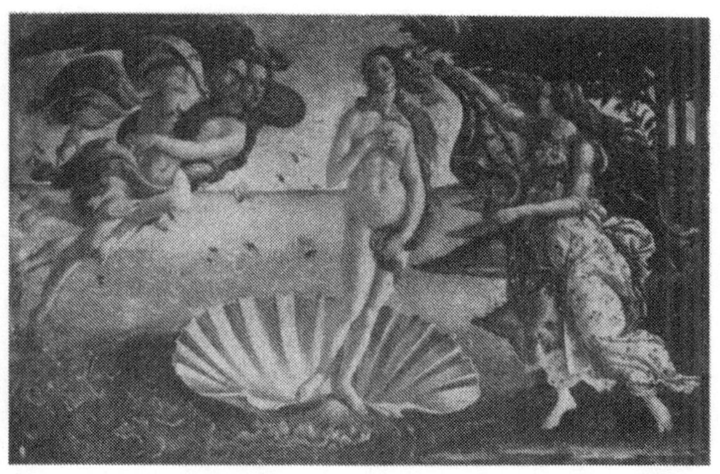

THE BIRTH OF VENUS   SANDRO BOTTICELLI

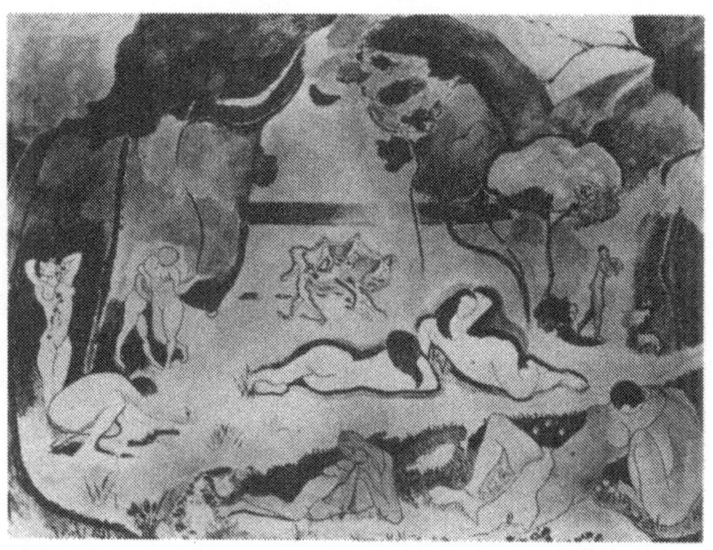

JOIE DE VIVRE   HENRI MATISSE

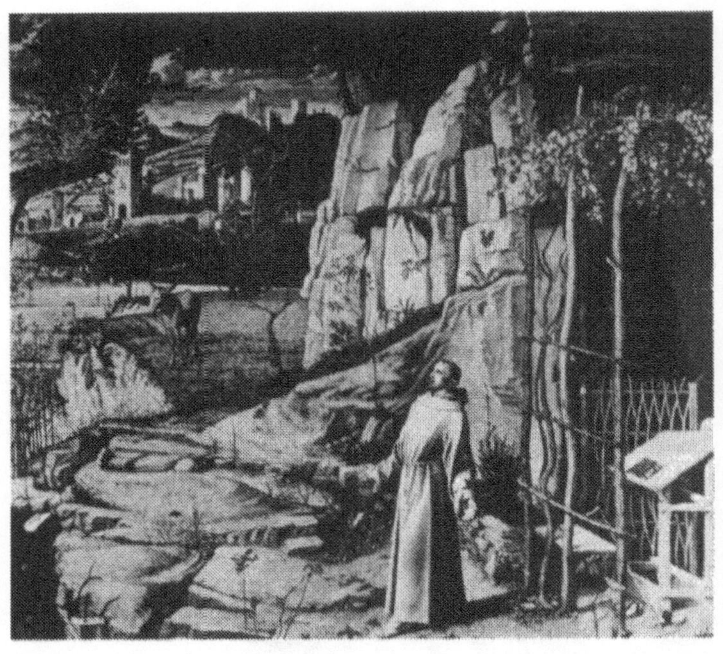

ST. FRANCIS IN ECSTASY   GIOVANNI BELLINI

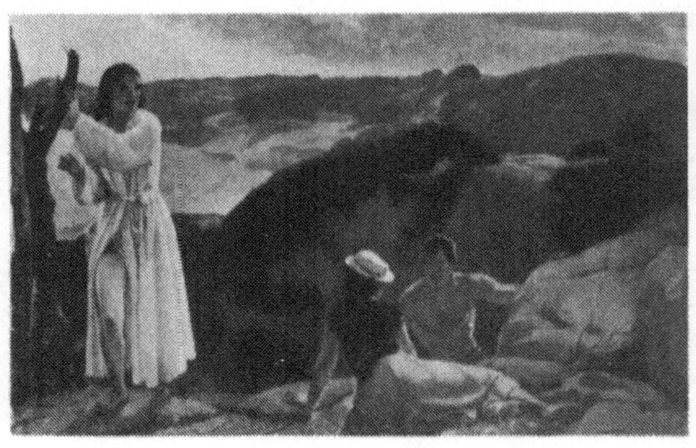

CAPE ANN   LEON KROLL

many cities), to arrive at an understanding of those principles upon which all art is firmly founded. For without an understanding of these all theory is useless; indeed, it is pernicious. Without this understanding a knowledge of the different styles and kinds of painting and sculpture is futile and leads, as we have seen, only to false estimates of an artist's works; for the various styles in art are merely ways of arriving at conclusions which embody these same principles. They are processes which, as Cézanne wisely said, "are nothing but simple methods for making the public feel what we ourselves feel, and for making ourselves intelligible."

If the layman and the student will see these things in their right relation they will also see that there are standards of judgment in art; standards which are always the same regardless of fashion, that art is not merely a matter of taste. When they see these things they will also see that unless a work embodies these principles first and last, it cannot be truly a work of art. These are the first and most important facts in art.

But, truly, these things are well known. They belong to the wisdom of the ages. Perhaps for this reason they have been so largely ignored in our time, or forgotten because of the urge to arrive by novel methods at an understanding of the nature of art. Theoretical analyses, "phoney profundities," which lend themselves so readily to verbal expression, immerse their victims in the complexity of detail and, thence, in the confusion of language.

.   .   .   .   .

We have seen, if briefly, that writing on art during the twentieth century has developed a system of analysis and criticism which is far removed from those problems which primarily concern the artist. We have seen that, in order to give non-traditional works a theoretically logical place in the realm of art, the traditional artist's aim has been falsified past all recognition; that his art has been termed mechanistic, scientific, impressionistic, imitative, material rather than spiritual; that he has had but one purpose—to reproduce exactly what the eye sees. Theorists say that the vitality of so limited a tradition is now exhausted and that it is natural that a reaction should have set in; that artists should have revolted from the constraint imposed upon them by such limitations. Therefore the non-traditional artist's pursuit of the spiritual and the abstract is a logical outcome of his revolt from outworn materialistic ideals.

But what theorists say is not borne out in the artist's works. We have seen that unintelligible form is simply unintelligible form. It is, today, no longer even a novelty, therefore theorists nowadays cannot seek refuge in the old cry that works whose form is unintelligible are misunderstood because they are new. Every conceivable explanation has been made for them but this has not rendered their form explicable.

We find upon examination of the non-traditional artist's avowed purpose that the search for more expressive form than has hitherto been known results only in form untrue to the artist's intention. That intention becomes verbal because he cannot master it in his own medium. Should there come a time when he can show himself master of his theories, his form will speak for itself; explanatory words will be unnecessary.

Hans Andersen's tale of the Emperor's New Clothes suggests a parable. Two rascals came to the Emperor. They called themselves master weavers and said their stuffs were unusually beautiful in color and pattern. But, greatest wonder of all, the stuffs were invisible to anyone unfit for his office or incorrigibly stupid. To test his court, the Emperor ordered a suit of clothes. The looms were set up and the weavers went through the motions of weaving but without making anything. Impatient, the Emperor sent first his trusted ministers, then his court, and finally went himself to inspect the weavers' progress. But no one, not even the Emperor himself, dared say that he could see nothing, for each feared to be thought incorrigibly stupid or unfit for his office. Instead they all fell in with the deception; the weavers appeared to dress the Emperor in the phantom clothes and the courtiers appeared to carry the train. They made a procession and marched through the town, acclaimed by a great crowd. Suddenly a child cried out, "But he has nothing on." The child's words were passed through the crowd and the whole people began to shout the same thing. And the Emperor shivered, for it seemed to him that they were right. But he said to himself that he must go through with the procession; and he carried himself still more proudly, and his chamberlains gripped still tighter the train which did not exist.

•   •   •   •   •

When words have said all that can be said about the art of the past and about twentieth-century non-traditional art, it must be self-evident that they fail in any degree to alter the meaning of the works themselves; that these state no more and no less than their own form has the power to convey; that where that form is used intelligibly the work is comprehensible and where it is not intelligibly used it fails to communicate the artist's idea.

In the preface we suggested that perhaps it were better to know nothing about art and to be able to say what one liked rather than that one's mind should be occupied with theories directing one's likes and dislikes. This is all very well, but in the end it is not enough—not, at least, for the intelligent observer, as doubtless he will agree. If he desires to know more of what he is enjoying he will find himself in perplexing circumstances because of all that he hears round about him. Nevertheless, if he will think before he speaks (rather than afterwards, or not at all), he may gain a knowledge of what it is he enjoys. For the verbal expression of his enjoyment will indicate the character of his pleasure—whether it is genuine enjoyment of true qualities in the work, whether these qualities are of the art or of the subject or whether his enjoyment reveals itself in a command of apt phrases with which he happily deceives himself, believing in all sincerity that his enjoyment lies in the work itself. When, for instance, he points out how the artist "has seen his work in terms of receding and advancing planes"; how he has "integrated cosmic forces in its plastic organization"; how it "expresses the spirit of his time" or how it embodies "new spatial values of color and texture"—when the observer speaks in such terms as these he is enjoying the sound of apt phrases and the mystery with which they fill his mind.

But the layman may protest all this, saying that if he enjoys the works of Matisse, Rousseau or Dali, this is sufficient reason in itself to warrant the thought that what is being enjoyed is worth while as art, and that if his knowing what he likes is to be a basis for cultivating a knowledge of art he must be confident that because he likes or enjoys these works they must have some claim to being works of art. There is one rejoinder to be made to this, and that is, that the liking and enjoyment of twentieth-century non-traditional works is invariably expressed in such phrases as have been noted in this book.

And the only possible excuse for giving serious consideration to such writings as have been reviewed in these pages is that the public has been asked to consider them seriously and to accept the kind of thought they contain as necessary to an understanding of the non-traditional artist's performance. But the conclusion to which a serious consideration of these writings has led is this: that we find they are composed of verbally expressed theories irrelevant to the principles of artistic creation and are, therefore, also irrelevant to any critical appreciation of the arts of painting and sculpture; that their authors are not in agreement as to the essential qualities which inform the product of which they treat, calling it at once formless and expressive of essential form; that the artist's form has been of the same intelligible, significant nature throughout the ages and in all manners and modes of presentation, but that it has lost significance and has become unintelligible in twentieth-century non-traditional works since it has, in itself, failed to convey the artist's intentions and needs the assistance of verbal explanation; and that, finally, a study of these works in combination with the literature they have called forth reveals beyond any doubt that the qualities which that literature exalts are chiefly remarkable for their absence in the works themselves. The only point in which both works and literature are consistent is in the evasion of those questions which should concern the artist.

To the eager student, absorbed in today's phantasmagoria, who thumbs the pages of the latest books on art till they are brown and worn, let it be said that the sooner he closes their covers and turns with his eyes to the observation of nature and a study of the works of the masters in painting and sculpture, the sooner will he liberate his mind and his spirit from the shackles of theory expressed in words.

Only with infinite patience and the love of the process of work may the youthful artist learn to understand the possibilities and the limitations of his medium and, through understanding, become a master of his art. If then he chooses to theorize he may do so to his own contentment without harm either to his own works or to the works of others.

For want of me the world's course will not fail;
When all its work is done the lie shall rot;
The truth is great and shall prevail,
When none cares whether it prevail or not.

COVENTRY PATMORE

ACKNOWLEDGMENTS

For permission to use selections the author is indebted to:

PUBLISHER	TITLE OF BOOK	AUTHOR
Coward-McCann		Roger Fry
	Vision and Design	
Ginn & Company		J. H. Breasted
	Ancient Times	
Barnes Foundation		Albert C. Barnes and Violette de Mazia
	The Art of Renoir	
Alfred A. Knopf		Gerstle Mack
	Paul Cézanne	
Faber and Faber		The Editors
	Circle	
Simon and Schuster		Thomas Craven
	Modern Art	
J. B. Lippincott		Theodore Duret
	Manet and the French Impressionists	
Harcourt, Brace and Company, Inc.		Herbert Read
	Art Now	
Harcourt, Brace and Company, Inc.		Albert C. Barnes
	The Art in Painting	
W. W. Norton & Company, Inc.		Mary Cecil Allen
	Painters of the Modern Mind	

PUBLISHER	TITLE OF BOOK	AUTHOR

W. W. Norton & Company, Inc.   Thomas Munro
Scientific Method in Aesthetics

Museum of Modern Art   Alfred H. Barr, Jr.
Cubism and Abstract Art

G. P. Putnam's Sons   John Dewey
Art as Experience

G. P. Putnam's Sons   Bernard Berenson
Florentine Painters of the Renaissance

Liveright Publishing Corporation   Sheldon Cheney
Expressionism in Art

The Atlantic Monthly Company   Bertrand Russell
Philosophy's Ulterior Motives

University of Chicago Press   Edward F. Rothschild
The Meaning of Unintelligibility in Modern Art

Les Editions G. Cres et Cie.   Ambroise Vollard
Paul Cézanne

BIBLIOGRAPHY

Art as Experience, John Dewey.
Art Now, Herbert Read.
Art and Society, Herbert Read.
The Art of Renoir, Albert C. Barnes and Violette de Mazia.
The Art in Painting, Albert C. Barnes.
Modern Art, Thomas Craven.
The Modern Movement in Art, R. H. Wilenski.
Meaning of Modern Sculpture, R. H. Wilenski.
The Meaning of Unintelligibility in Modern Art, Edward F. Rothschild.
Expressionism in Art, Sheldon Cheney.
Cubism and Abstract Art, Alfred H. Barr, Jr.
Du "Cubisme," Albert Gleizes and Jean Metzinger.
Circle, Editors, J. L. Martin, Ben Nicholson, N. Gabo.
Painters of the Modern Mind, Mary Cecil Allen.
The Mirror of the Passing World, Mary Cecil Allen.
Vision and Design, Roger Fry.
Modern Artists, Christian Brinton.
How to Study the Modern Painters, Charles H. Caffin.
Manet and the French Impressionists, Theodore Duret.
The French Impressionists, Camille Mauclair.
Paul Cézanne, Gerstle Mack.
Paul Cézanne, Ambroise Vollard.
Paul Cézanne, Correspondance recueillie, annotée et prefacée by John Rewald.
Cézanne, Lionello Venturi.
Cézanne, Roger Fry.
Cézanne, Gustave Coquiot.

Cézanne, George Rivière.
Gauguin, Charles Kunstler.
Seurat, Daniel Cotton Rich.
Henri Matisse, Intro. Alfred H. Barr, Jr., with notes by the artist.
After Picasso, James Thrall Soby.
Ancient Times, James Henry Breasted.
Art Throughout the Ages, Helen Gardner.
A World History of Art, Sheldon Cheney.
Reynolds' Discourses, Intro. and Notes by Roger Fry.
Leonardo da Vinci's Note Books, Edward McCurdy.
The Book of the Art of Cennino Cennini, Christiana J. Herringham.
The Materials of Medieval Painting, Daniel V. Thompson, Jr.
The Journal of Eugene Delacroix, Trans. Walter Pach.
Stones of Venice, John Ruskin.
The Florentine Painters of the Renaissance, Bernard Berenson.
Ancient Painting, M. H. Swindler.
History of Art Criticism, Lionello Venturi.
Critical History of Modern Aesthetics, Earl of Listowel.
Scientific Method in Aesthetics, Thomas Munro.
Art for Art's Sake, Albert Guérard.
The Sense of Beauty, George Santayana.
The Higher Life in Art, John La Farge.
Aesthetic Judgment, D. W. Prall.
Form and Color, L. March Phillipps.
Dialogues of Plato, B. Jowett.
Select Passages from the Introductions to Plato, Benjamin Jowett.
Aristotle on the Art of Poetry, Lane Cooper.
Aristotle's Theory of Poetry and Fine Art, S. H. Butcher.
Conway Letters, The Correspondence of Anne, Viscountess Conway, etc., Marjorie Hope Nicholson.

Magazines

"Cézanne," *L'Occident*, Juillet 1904, Émile Bernard.

"Souvenirs sur Paul Cézanne et Lettres," *A La Renova-tion Esthetique* (no date), Émile Bernard.

"Souvenirs sur Paul Cézanne," *Mercure de France*, October 1907, Émile Bernard.

"Une Conversation Avec Cézanne," *Mercure de France*, June 1921, Émile Bernard.

"Philosophy's Ulterior Motives," *The Atlantic Monthly*, February, 1936, Bertrand Russell.

EU Authorised Representative:
Easy Access System Europe
Mustamäe tee 50, 10621 Tallinn, Estonia

www.ingramcontent.com/pod-product-compliance
Lightning Source LLC
Chambersburg PA
CBHW022207050726
47590CB00002B/685